DRIVING WITH A

TEENAGE BRAIN

DRIVING WITH A
TEENAGE BRAIN

A State Trooper's Notes
On How To Stay Alive

Richard Kasper

Published by:

Richard Kasper

drivingwithateenagebrain@gmail.com

Cover photo courtesy of Coeur d'Alene Press, Coeur d'Alene, Idaho

Cover design and illustrations by Chris Kasper

Printed in the USA

Copies may be purchased at Amazon.com

ISBN-13: 978-1978219250

ISBN-10: 1978219253

ACKNOWLEDGEMENT

A special thanks to the following law enforcement professionals for their time and expertise in reviewing and commenting on this book.

Investigating traffic accidents - especially those resulting in death or serious physical injury - is one of the most difficult jobs facing a police officer. When those accidents involve young or inexperienced drivers, the task is especially agonizing. With an emphasis upon driver safety, this very comprehensive book is an excellent resource for teenagers and parents alike, and I highly recommend it!
Daniel Carlson - Captain, Assistant Director of Training, New York State Police, Ret.

Rich, thanks for letting me review your book. It's obvious you put a lot of effort into it, drawing on your unique experiences. I especially liked your personal stories and all of your common sense, practical advice! You have provided an informative life-saving guide for everyone hoping to avoid a motor vehicle accident. I am confident you will make better, more thoughtful drivers with your insights. Each of my own grandchildren will be receiving a copy of this book as they prepare to get behind the wheel and hit the road. Excellent job!
Lars Jarvie - Chief of Police, City of Mesa, Arizona, Ret.

Richard Kasper has developed a common-sense guide for those who don't always use a great deal of common sense. I wish that this book existed when my sons were learning to drive. Nicely done!
Ben Wolfinger - Sheriff, Kootenai County, Idaho

Great information even for me, an old retired cop of 34 years. Having raised five children and worked with youth in Boy Scouts and church activities, I can attest that, while they are wonderful people, teenagers act like teenagers. The information in this book may save a teen's life. Thanks for writing this, Rich. I will share it with my kids.

Gordon H. Gartner - Chief of Police, Town of Payson, Arizona, Ret.

Dedication

For my beautiful grandchildren

and

teenage drivers everywhere

TABLE OF CONTENTS

ABOUT THE AUTHOR

WHEN THE AUTHOR was 18 years old, he narrowly escaped a head-on automobile accident. Then, at 20, he was in a serious crash when a drunk, driving the wrong way, hit him head-on. These two incidents gave him a life-long desire to learn the safest driving techniques and to drive the safest vehicles.

The author's professional driver training began as a trooper with the New York State Police. As part of his duties he investigated more than 1,100 motor vehicle accidents, many involving serious injuries and death. In addition to determining the cause of each accident, he had the opportunity to observe the crashworthiness of hundreds of vehicles of various sizes and designs.

After 10 years, he attended law school. He practiced law for four years and then returned to police work as a legal advisor and academy instructor at the Mesa Police Department in Arizona. He kept abreast of the latest accident avoidance techniques by practicing alongside the officers on the academy driving track. The techniques described herein, along with a little luck, have enabled him to drive almost 900,000 accident-free miles since that head-on crash.

INTRODUCTION

It happened in a small farming community, on a warm summer evening, in rural New York State. It was an area of family dairy farms set in rolling hills. The weather was clear and the roadway dry. Traffic was very light, almost non-existent. I remember a soft breeze and the sound of crickets. I can still picture the beautiful teenaged girl, lying still in the roadway. She looked peaceful, as if she were just looking up at the stars, or perhaps counting the fireflies and listening to the sounds of the night. But she wasn't seeing or hearing anything. Poor choices, easily avoided, caused her death. It was the tragic result of an accident that should never have happened.

Motor vehicle crashes are the leading cause of death for teenagers of driving age. Based on miles driven, they are involved in three times the number of fatal crashes as any other age group. There are numerous reasons for this heartbreaking fact. Lack of maturity and experience are two. Maturity will come with time. Experience can be gained, in the safest environment possible, if certain techniques and suggestions are followed. But I believe a major factor in teen fatalities is risk-taking behavior. That part of the human brain that gives us the ability to judge risk is not yet fully developed in the teen brain. The good news is that these risk-taking behaviors can be recognized and eliminated.

Teens aren't required to have adequate experience in, or information about, the safest driving techniques to obtain a driver's license. If a teen can pass a short driving test and has some knowledge of local driving laws, it is enough to get a driving permit, and eventually a license. But it is not enough to survive the early driving years. Teens need a lot more information about every aspect of driving than what is currently required.

This book started out as a collection of driving tips for my oldest granddaughter as she approached driving age. These tips could then be passed on to my granddaughter's siblings as they began to drive. I read several driving books hoping to find one to include with my thoughts. None of the driving books I found included all the factors I knew to be important. Most of them assumed a certain level of knowledge and experience that new drivers do not have. Instead of just a collection of miscellaneous notes, I decided to write a driving manual for my grandchildren.

Recalling that accident scene with the young girl lying in the roadway gave me the motivation to make this book available for all teen drivers. There is a lot of information here. Reading through it once will probably not be enough for you to understand and remember it all. It wouldn't have been for me when I was a novice driver. Keep it handy and reread it occasionally. It will help to keep you safe.

Chapter 1

YOUR PHYSICAL CONDITION

THE TEEN BRAIN

IN THE LAST 12 YEARS or so, neuroscientists, using magnetic resonance imaging, have been able to look inside the living brain and track its development. They have uncovered significant differences between the adult and teen brains. Teens are capable of being bright, clever, and accomplished. They can learn new languages and become skilled musicians more quickly and more easily than adults. They can also be impulsive, irrational and recklessly flaunt danger. Why would an intelligent and accomplished teen act impulsively and recklessly? Why do teens sometimes do the things we adults find so perplexing? It may well be your "unfinished" brain.

The physical size of your brain was completed when you were between 11 (girls) and 14 (boys) years of age. Sorry guys. But it does explain some of my youthful ignorance when around young girls my age. Even though the size of your brain has reached its adult proportions, all the internal connections won't be completed until well after your teen years. The limbic portion of your brain is the first to be completed. The amygdala is found here and is responsible for emotional and reactive behavior. It becomes super-charged in puberty. Have you ever heard of the phrase "Freeze, Flight or Fight"? It refers to your potential reaction when faced with an immediate danger. You will either freeze (do nothing), flee, or fight. Your choice would be an emotional, not a reasoned, reaction. That is your amygdala in action. You don't want that when you are driving.

The last part of the brain to be completed is found in the pre-frontal cortex. As the name implies, it is in the front of the brain. You use this portion of your brain for making thoughtful and logical decisions. It provides sound judgment and controls impulses. It is responsible for planning, reasoning and logic. It gives you the ability to imagine hypothetical situations – to consider past, present and future outcomes based on differing choices. This part of your brain won't be completed until you are in your middle to late twenties. As a teen, your choices will tend to be guided by your emotional and reactive amygdala rather than by your thoughtful and logical pre-frontal cortex. You can still make thoughtful and logical decisions. It just takes a bit longer. You have the brain – you just don't have all the internal scaffolding. What you don't want is for the impulsive portion of your brain to react when driving, before your logical pre-frontal cortex can offer an alternative. How can you do this with your incomplete brain? Like most any other problem you will be faced with in life, once you understand the problem, you are halfway to a solution. By pre-thinking, pre-planning and pre-deciding what to do in certain driving situations, you will have added the other half of the solution. You can train your brain to choose the best and safest way to react when faced with a potentially hazardous driving situation. That is primarily what this book is about.

There will be many times while driving when you will be faced with a choice. Whenever there is a choice of whether to do one thing or the other, you need to choose the safer alternative. Don't rely on your incomplete pre-frontal cortex to judge risk versus reward. Training your brain to always choose the safer alternative eliminates the time it might take to reason it out, or the need to rely on your limbic system.

Imagine you are in town approaching a green traffic light. There are two lanes in each direction and traffic is medium to heavy. While you are still within stopping distance the light turns to yellow. You have room to stop but if you step on the gas pedal you believe you can make the light. What do you do? Did you have time to look both ways to be sure that all traffic in the cross streets is stopped? Are the crosswalks clear of pedestrians? Are there any bicyclists about that might move into your lane? Do you know how long the yellow light will stay on in this intersection? Don't even try to reason out the risks and rewards. Stopping is safer. You have told your subconscious that it is safer to stop in these situations and that is what you will do. You will not waste time on decision making. Your foot will be on the brake without even thinking about it.

Here is another example. Imagine that you are on a two-lane highway in a rural area, one lane each way, separated by a double yellow line. You are behind a vehicle traveling five miles under the speed limit. It is daytime, the weather is clear and the traffic is relatively light. The road is typical for the country – meandering curves with not a whole lot of straight roadway. You are in a hurry. You want to pass. You finally see the center line has changed to allow passing. There are two other vehicles behind you. They also probably want to pass. But you can't see far enough to be sure that you can pass before the passing lane ends unless you really "gun it". Then you can make it, probably. Do you pass? Do you stay where you are? What is the safer decision? If you stay where you are it might take a while longer to get where you are going. But you will not risk a head-on crash, or not being able to get back into your lane before the passing zone ends. A simple decision, isn't it?

You will learn how to train your brain, your subconscious, to always help you to make the safer decision. Lots of drivers will push the envelope when driving. They shouldn't. You shouldn't. Driving is a life and death matter. Your goal is to arrive at your destination safely, even if a bit late. You will be much later if you need to complete an accident report, get your vehicle towed, or be medically evacuated.

It may turn out that this difference in the teen brain, the unfinished pre-frontal cortex, is why so many teens are involved in fatal auto accidents. Their judgment of risk versus reward skills are not yet fully developed. Always choose the safer alternative. When you are twenty-five or so, your fully-completed pre-frontal cortex will applaud you.

RESTED AND ALERT

Driving can be a dangerous matter. You need to be in top physical condition – rested and alert. There are many legal, illegal and over- the-counter drugs that can affect your various senses. Some, like allergy pills, can make you drowsy. Others can affect your reasoning ability, lower your inhibitions, and/or increase your willingness to take risks. Alcohol comes to mind but there are others.

A little discussion about drinking and driving is in order here. According to the National Highway Traffic Safety

Administration (NHTSA), teens are at far greater risk of death in an alcohol-related crash than the overall population, despite the fact that they are below the minimum drinking age in every state. Every drink of an alcoholic beverage will affect your driving skills. While the legal limit of alcohol in your bloodstream varies from .08 to .10 in the states where I have lived, this is way too much in my experience.

The really-drunk driver will be easy to spot − he will be driving slowly and wandering about the lanes. If he drives fast he will not go very far before crashing. It is the slightly tipsy driver that poses the greatest hazard. He will be sober enough to drive fast, and often will do so, but his recognition of, and response to, the unexpected will be poor. He will be able to drive reasonably well, if he is on a familiar road, as long as nothing unexpected occurs. The unexpected will include normal driving situations that, when sober, wouldn't pose a problem. Here is an example: The tipsy driver approaches a green traffic light but it changes to red before he reaches the intersection. He doesn't anticipate that it might change, although he normally would. His failure to anticipate the light change creates a hazard that wouldn't have occurred had he been sober. His recognition of the light change and reaction to it is delayed. As a result, he runs the light.

Most of the worst drunk-driving accidents I investigated involved drivers that were somewhere around the legal blood/alcohol limit. What you might call slightly intoxicated. They weren't always legally "driving under the influence", but they were impaired enough so that they made poor driving decisions. Any alcoholic drink will impair everyone to some degree. A person doesn't go from totally sober to intoxicated only after a certain amount of alcohol. Impairment is a sliding scale that starts out with any amount of alcohol and moves up to legally intoxicated and beyond. Every drink has an effect.

So, no drinking and driving. Any drug, of whatever type, may have an effect on your driving ability as well. Until you know what that effect will be, be safe and don't drive. Of course, don't ride with another driver who is impaired due to alcohol or any drug.

No driving when you are tired, either. The following is a real-life example of the danger of driving while tired.

> *My partner and I were on patrol on a Friday about midnight. We stopped a young college student who had been driving on a two-lane roadway. His vehicle would first drive over the double yellow line and then wander over to and across the white shoulder line.*

His speed wasn't particularly fast. We stopped him. There was a second college student asleep in the back seat. It was apparent the driver was very tired. He had put in a full day at his studies and then had driven a little over 360 miles. He had another 100 or so miles to go to get home. He had no symptoms of drug or alcohol use so we gave him a choice, as we weren't going to let him continue to drive. He could either receive a ticket and a visit to a judge, or he could surrender his keys till 7am and get some sleep. He chose to give up his keys. The next morning, at the end of our shift, we returned his keys. He promised he would no longer drive when tired.

The very next Friday night, at about midnight, we responded to an accident no more than one-half mile from where we had stopped the students. Upon arrival, we saw the student's car smashed up against a tree. The young man had been killed instantly. A later autopsy showed no drugs or alcohol. His friend, who had again been sleeping in the back seat, survived. He admitted that they were both tired when they began their drive home.

I don't know how better to tell you of the danger of driving when you aren't well rested.

MAINTAINING A CALM DEMEANOR

Just as you need to be well rested and in good physical condition, you also need to be calm and in control of your emotions.

I assume that at any given time ten percent of drivers around me are a hazard to me. I expect that another driver will do something which will create an unnecessary risk. When such an event happens, and it will, I can remain calm, at least until the danger is passed. After all I was expecting it. This presumption about other drivers helps me to stay focused.

When another driver poses a threat, you need to remain calm to make the best decision to minimize the danger. If you become frightened enough, your brain will enter the "Freeze, Flight or Fight" mode. When this happens the reasoning portion of your brain, the pre-frontal cortex, shuts down. Your brain goes into auto pilot. You will either freeze, take flight or fight. You don't want this. If you "freeze" you will hesitate to take corrective action. You may fail to take any action at all. Taking "flight" might be a good response but you may not be able to do so. You may want to "fight" by doing something to that driver, such as cutting him off. A bad idea. Don't respond to aggressive drivers by doing something that might

9

make the situation worse. Just move out of their way when it is safe to do so.

In the movie Top Gun, one of the fighter pilots had the nickname "Iceman" because he never got stressed when in combat. He didn't panic. He maintained a calm demeanor. This helped to make him a Top Gun. I am sure that actual combat pilots must have this skill. I liked this "Iceman" mental attitude. I do my best to emulate it. Not only for driving, but for other situations that require good focus. Archery competition and poker come to mind. I enjoy both but either can be stressful. Having that control of my emotions helps me to make the best decisions. It will be of great value to you as well. Promise yourself that, no matter what happens when driving, you will remain calm. By continually telling yourself that you will remain calm in the face of danger you are training your brain to keep you calm. You can do this.

In another chapter I address visualization, a method to mentally prepare yourself for unexpected, potentially dangerous situations without having to experience them. That will also help to keep you calm when the unexpected does occur.

STAYING FOCUSED

Ten percent of drivers under the age of 20 involved in fatal motor vehicle accidents were reported to have been distracted at the time of the crash. The following incident happened to me just a few years ago.

I was stopped at a traffic light a few hundred yards from an elementary school. It was the first day of school. There was a crossing guard a little further away at a much busier intersection but no crossing guard at my intersection. A small boy entered the crosswalk from my left. He appeared to be five, no more than six years old. He was alone and carrying a metal lunchbox. As he passed in front of my truck I could no longer see him. I waited for him to appear to the right of my truck but he did not. The light changed to green. I put the truck in park and quickly got out to stop any traffic that might be approaching from behind, and to look for him. He was sitting on the ground directly in front of my bumper, crying. His lunchbox was open on the ground and a sandwich and an apple were lying next to it. I am sure I would have seriously injured him, or worse, had I been

> *distracted and not watching. I still get a bad feeling when I think about that day.*

Driving a vehicle is a great responsibility. You are moving around a few tons of metal, plastic and rubber. While other drivers can pose a threat to your safety, your vehicle is also a potential hazard to others. Stay focused on your driving and on your surroundings while behind the wheel, whether moving or just stopped. Don't allow yourself to be distracted. Later, we will talk about being aware of everything in your "bubble" – that area surrounding you, from which a hazard might arise.

MULTITASKING

This is a no-no. Multitasking causes distractions. When driving, you sometimes need to multi-task. An example would be trying to decide what exit to take while also consciously trying to stay in your own lane. With experience, staying in your own lane, along with other common driving skills, will be pretty much handled by your subconscious. But distractions cause accidents. As an inexperienced driver, you need to keep them to the minimum.

There are three separate types of distractions that will affect your concentration on driving. Anything that takes your eyes from where you should be looking is a **visual distraction**.

Looking at your passenger instead of where you are driving is an example. Anything that takes your mind from your driving is a **cognitive distraction**. Thinking about what you are going to say in response to a question would be a cognitive distraction. Studies have shown that talking on a phone, even hands-free, causes more of a distraction than talking to a person in the vehicle. Perhaps doing so requires more concentration. Using your hand or hands to text would be a **manual distraction**. Texting, as well as using phone apps and the internet, while driving, involves all three types of distractions. This is what makes it so deadly. The National Highway Safety Traffic Administration (NHTSA) has stated that distractions cause about 20% of all accidents. They also found that phone usage while driving will increase your chances of having an accident by 23 times! Recent studies reported that over the last four decades, highway fatalities had steadily declined. However, with the introduction of car Wi-Fi and many new apps, highway fatalities in the year 2015 increased by the largest annual percentage in 50 years!

An NHTSA study involved interviewing teens in several states. Self-caused distractions were mentioned frequently by the teens. Having friends in the car was the most common distraction. Changing the radio station and talking on a cell phone were mentioned often. Eating and singing were others. Having the radio on loud, eliminating any possibility of hearing other traffic, was yet another. Some admitted to wrestling with friends. Some said arguing with friends was a common distraction – more girls than boys admitted to this. Some girls in the focus group acknowledged the dangers of distractions caused by friends. However, they still opposed placing limits on the number of friends they would be allowed to have in the car. Do you suppose this is due to their unfinished pre-frontal cortex affecting their judgment?

Most of the teens believed they could handle distractions and still be safe drivers. They can't. You can't. Every distraction, to every driver, increases the risk of an accident. Any distraction makes you a less safe driver- at greater risk of an accident. Eliminate all optional distractions. Save your talking, texting, arguing, eating and all other risky behaviors for when you are neither a driver nor a passenger.

There are times when you must multitask when driving. Looking away from the roadway at a traffic sign is an example of a visual distraction. Assuming you are driving, you would be multitasking. Hopefully it will only be for a split second. Even this can cause problems.

Just a few months ago, while traveling along on a freeway in Mesa, Arizona, an overhead, lighted sign warned of an accident a few miles ahead. It also suggested leaving the freeway at a specific exit. As one vehicle in the next lane to my right slowed, apparently for the driver to read the entire message, another vehicle ran into the first from behind. I imagine that the second driver was reading the warning as well. Kind of ironic – a warning of an accident which created a situation that resulted in another one. The sign only created the distraction, it did not cause the accident. Both drivers were at fault, the first by not watching for traffic behind when slowing down and the second by not watching in front and following too closely.

If you are driving in a familiar area, you will take little time to read signs. You will already know what most of them say. However, those drivers around you, who are not as familiar with the area will take longer to read them. They will be multitasking longer than a split second. Anytime a driver is multitasking there is an increased chance of an accident. Keep them to a minimum for yourself. Don't add any unnecessary distractions while driving.

FOOTWEAR

Seems like a strange subject for driving tips, doesn't it? Some footwear can affect your ability to use the brake pedal. Never a good thing. Loose fitting flip flops as well as some sandals can do this. When you move your foot from the gas pedal to the brake, if the front of the flip flop or sandal is caught under the brake pedal while your foot is moving onto the pedal, you may not be able to get more than your toes onto the pedal. If that happens you will be unable to press the pedal as hard as you might need to. Also, no bare feet. If a pebble is either stuck on your foot or on the brake pedal, your automatic response will be to pull your foot off the pedal. Not a good idea if you were planning to stop. You don't have to wear combat boots, just something that won't cause braking problems.

SUNGLASSES

If you wear sunglasses, save your money to get a good pair that are polarized. They eliminate glare from the hood, windshield and other vehicles. They make it easier to see and they decrease eye strain. Remember to take them off when going through tunnels and at sundown.

Chapter 2

KNOWING YOUR VEHICLE

READ THE OPERATOR'S MANUAL. It should explain the safety features in the vehicle and where each control is located. Does it have anti-lock brakes? A vehicle stability control system? A passive or active collision avoidance system? New safety features are being added all the time. Some give audible, visual and/or tactile warnings (vibrating steering wheel or driver's seat). Others may apply the brakes or control the steering. You need to understand which electronic safety features your vehicle has, what they do, and how each will assist with your driving.

The glossary at the end of this manual includes explanations for the more common terms and acronyms.

If you learn to drive one vehicle but occasionally drive another, you need to familiarize yourself with that vehicle's controls. While the steering wheel, brake and gas pedals will be in the same place, other controls will vary. On one of my vehicles, the controls for the radio and cruise control are at my fingertips while my hands are on the wheel, on my other, the controls located there are a second set of shift controls for the transmission, allowing gear changes without removing my hands from the steering wheel. You wouldn't want to confuse the two.

Every vehicle you will drive will be somewhat different than all the others. Even two vehicles which are the same model and year may have different options with different or additional controls. Make sure that you are comfortable with the controls and the electronic systems before driving off.

PRE-DRIVING CHECK

Walkabout

Take a quick look around the vehicle to ensure it looks OK. No serious oil or other leaks. If you see clear water on the ground under the engine compartment it is from the air conditioning unit. This is normal if the vehicle has been driven recently. Any other leaks might indicate a problem. One or two drops probably won't indicate a problem requiring immediate attention but any large puddle of a colored liquid indicates a problem that needs immediate attention. Give the tires a brief look to see if the tires are inflated properly. There should be a small bulge at side of the tire where it meets the ground. All four tires should have the same amount of bulge. Sometime, when you know that the tires are inflated properly, notice the size of the bulge. It won't be very large.

Then, every time before entering the vehicle, give the tires a quick glance. You don't want to drive off on an under-inflated or flat tire. This walkabout will only take a few seconds. It just may save you from being stranded with a disabled vehicle later.

Seat Adjustment

Adjust the seat until you can reach the brake and gas pedals while your knee is still bent and your back is against the seat back. Move the seat up/down so you can reach the steering wheel with your elbows slightly bent. If your vehicle has an adjustable steering wheel, now is the time to adjust it. You should be able to see over your right shoulder towards the right rear of the vehicle. This is the "blind spot" where it can be difficult to see a vehicle just off your right rear tire. Many vehicles now have power seats and movable steering columns that will make these adjustments easy. You should be comfortable and not have to reach, either with your feet or your hands. Unless you are driving a manual, or "stick" shift vehicle, your left foot won't have any work to do. It should rest lightly on the floorboard. If it doesn't, adjust the seat so it does. This will make your driving experience more comfortable.

Mirror Adjustment

Adjust the left outside mirror so that you can see the complete lane on your left. If your vehicle has a good-sized mirror, you will also be able to see about another half or more of the second lane on your left. Adjust it so that for you to see the door handle on your door you must move your head about six to ten inches to the left. Do not adjust it to see the side of the vehicle. Doing so will cut off too much of the adjoining lane. You should be able to see a vehicle approaching you in the lane to your left in the rear-view mirror and then in the left side mirror with a smooth transition. There should be no gap where you cannot see it. This is especially important to enable you to see motorcycles as well. The mirror on the right will be convex. This allows you to see the entire lane to the right which would not be possible if the glass was flat like the left mirror. However, the drawback is, as noted on the mirror, objects in the mirror will be closer than they appear. This difference in depth of view between the right and left mirrors can be deceptive.

Adjust the rear-view mirror so you can see straight back. Remove any obstructions to your view in all directions. Sometimes rear seat headrests can cut off part of your view to the right rear and to the back. It there are no passengers in those seats remove them if possible, or at least lower them.

In some vehicles, they fold forward. There should be no window stickers that could obstruct your view. Also, remove any items in your view that might distract you, such as items dangling from the rear-view mirror.

Check Lights and Turn Signals

Keep headlights and taillights clean and clear. Check that headlights, both high and low, are all working. Insure that all turn signals, parking/running lights and taillights are working. You will sometimes use headlights during daylight hours so it is always a good idea to check them. After a while, you won't always check these items every time you get in the vehicle. However, if it has been a while since you have done so, go ahead and do it.

Windshield and Windows

Windshields tend to collect grime as well as just plain dirt and bugs. They should be clean inside and out. Also, keep all other windows and outside mirrors clean. Glare from other vehicle lights and street lights can make an otherwise clean window look hazy. It is a good idea when gassing up to clean the windshield, and any other windows that might need it. Also, when cleaning the windshield, clean the wipers as well. They also tend to collect grime. Cleaning them occasionally with alcohol or vinegar helps. Check their operation. If there is snow or ice on the windows, clean them all, not just the windshield. I know, it makes sense, why would I even mention it? I once saw someone driving a snow-covered car with a basketball sized spot on the windshield cleared. The rest of the windshield and all other windows were covered with snow. That person may be a statistic by now. Remember to clean the turn signals and taillights of snow and ice as well.

Controls

Before you drive off you need to know where all the controls are, not just the brake, accelerator and steering wheel. You need to know the location of each so you won't have to look for them while driving.

Learn how to operate the turn signals, the emergency four-way flashers, the windshield wipers and washers. How do you turn on the headlights and running lights? Are they automatic or do you need to turn them on? How about the climate controls? You should know where the radio and cruise controls are. You shouldn't use either until you are a somewhat seasoned driver but you should know where they are so you don't accidentally turn them on while reaching for something else. The mirror adjustments should be made before driving off but you may find that you need to readjust them once on the road, particularly the side view mirrors.

Before you drive off, practice adjusting them while looking out the windshield as if you were driving. Can you adjust the steering wheel up/down, in/out? Some vehicles offer both adjustments while others do not. Make these adjustments before driving off.

Loose/Dangerous Objects/Cargo

Do not leave any heavy or hard objects in the passenger compartment. Store them in the trunk or secure them. Drivers and passengers have been seriously injured and some killed in accidents when loose objects have struck them. Think about it. If you travel at 50 miles an hour and have an accident any loose object on the back seat would also be traveling 50 miles an hour. On impact your vehicle would be either stopped or traveling at a reduced speed. The loose object would still be traveling at fifty miles an hour. If it hits someone, imagine the damage it could cause.

In one accident, a concrete block, put on the floor behind the driver's seat for extra weight when driving in snow, struck the driver in the head. In another, a loose camera struck the driver and caused a serious head injury in addition to the injuries from the accident.

Unrestrained animals can also become dangerous flying objects in an accident. For your safety and that of your pet secure them properly. Do not let a pet sit on your lap or anywhere else unrestrained. No gasoline containers should be in the passenger compartment. Even empty ones contain explosive fumes. It isn't a good idea to have them in the trunk either.

Passengers

Require all passengers to wear seat belts – no exceptions. Insure that children are in appropriate child restraints. However, you shouldn't be driving with children or even passengers, other than your parent or trainer, until you become an experienced driver.

Brakes

Check to make sure they are working. With the vehicle running, and before driving off, step on the brake pedal. It should depress to a certain point and then stop. It should not fade slowly to the floor. If it does, don't drive until it is fixed. Vehicles are becoming more reliable with each new model so you probably will never experience this problem. It is a still a good safety check.

Gas

Make sure you have enough to get wherever it is you are going. Sounds simple but some friends of mine crashed a small plane because no one checked the gas level before taking off. Fortunately, all survived with just a few minor injuries due to the pilot's skill. Running out of gas in a vehicle probably wouldn't be as exciting but still not fun.

Distractions

Turn off stereos, etc. Place cell phone out of reach if you can't ignore it while driving. Take care of all phone calls, texts, etc. before starting the vehicle. You will have plenty to do while learning to drive safely. You cannot afford to be distracted.

Chapter 3

BASIC "HOW TO MOVE A VEHICLE" SKILLS

USING THE GAS PEDAL

PERHAPS THIS WILL BE called the "go" pedal for electric cars. Accelerate smoothly. No need to floor the gas pedal unless in an emergency. When making a stop, let up on the gas pedal well before the stop. In town, anticipate the need for the next stop to allow for a gradual slowing down rather than a hard, lurching stop.

USING THE BRAKE PEDAL

Braking

In a normal, non-emergency situation, brake smoothly. Apply the brake softly, increasing the pressure gradually until almost stopped, then continually lessen the pressure as you are approaching the stop. It should be difficult for a passenger with her eyes closed to tell exactly when you have completely stopped. Practice this in a parking lot or other no-traffic area.

Learning to accelerate and brake smoothly will not only save gas but will also contribute to a comfortable ride.

Braking for An Intersection Turn

Put your turn signal on to alert other drivers of your intention. The goal here is to do almost all braking before the turn. Apply them well before the turn and continue braking no more than 1/3 into the turn. Then slowly apply the gas pedal at the end of the turn. Using the gas pedal to complete the turn rather than just coasting through will give better control of the vehicle. The timing of the turn would be approximately one third braking, then moving your foot to the gas pedal and then slowly accelerating.

Braking in A Turn Other Than at An Intersection

We will address the physics of vehicle movement in another section of this book. For now, you just need to understand that when braking in a turn there is a greater chance of losing the traction of one or more tires and causing a skid, than when braking in a straight line. Going downhill and braking in a turn increases this likelihood. A wet or snowy road surface increases the chances of a skid. To minimize this problem, brake or downshift before the turn as much as possible. You can still brake through part of the turn but you don't want to be in a position where you must brake hard in any turn.

Braking in An Emergency

Step on the pedal hard and keep the pressure on until the emergency is over. All modern vehicles have, or should have, anti-lock brakes (ABS) and some form of vehicle stability control (VSC). See the glossary for an explanation of these terms. The ABS system will apply and release each wheel brake many times a second. The VSC system will apply braking to each wheel individually, as needed, to prevent under or over steer. Some VSC systems also will reduce engine power. ABS and VSC combined will help to avoid skids and loss of directional control. No matter what the emergency is, don't ever make large steering wheel adjustments at highway speeds. Just step hard on the brake pedal and, if necessary, make a small steering wheel adjustment.

STEERING

The current advice is to place your hands at the nine and three o'clock positions. Previously the recommendation was the 10 and two o'clock positions. But when air bags were added to the steering column the advice changed. I use either depending upon how the steering wheel is designed. Keep your thumbs along the wheel, not wrapped around. Your grip should be relaxed with slightly bent elbows. It takes very little movement of the wheel to move the vehicle in another direction. At highway speeds, you will need only to move the wheel an inch or so to change lanes. When turning a corner at low speeds, as in town, you will be driving just a few miles an hour. When making these turns you will make large movements of the wheel, perhaps turning the wheel 180 degrees or so. If you did this at highway speeds you would go into a skid and possibly turn over. Not a good thing. You will quickly learn how much to turn the wheel in each situation when you practice in a non-traffic situation.

When making a turn, slide one hand up to the other and then slide the other further along the wheel, rather than hand over hand.   While maneuvering through a parking lot or negotiating slow turns in town, it may be more comfortable to use a hand over hand method. For slow, in town turns I let the wheel return by slightly loosening my grip on the wheel and letting it slide through my fingers until mostly straight. Then I finish the turn by turning the wheel. This takes some getting used to and will have a different feel for each vehicle. You will decide which is the most practical for you. Just be sure that whatever method you use you still have control of the wheel at all times. At any speed above slow, use the sliding hand method.

On long drives, it may become necessary to change hand positions to reduce hand fatigue. I will move them around somewhat. I have even used twelve or one o'clock with the right hand and seven o'clock with the left on long drives. I still have control with either hand as not much movement of the wheel is necessary at highway speeds. I use this only when traffic is very light or non-existent. The key here is to have both hands on the wheel. Remember, no large movements of the wheel at highway speeds, ever. I will stress this again. Large movements of the steering wheel at highway speeds is the cause of many accidents.

If you encounter some unexpected road debris or an animal, grip the wheel firmly and try to move out of the way, braking if necessary. Make small wheel movements only. If you cannot move completely out of the way with small steering adjustments, running into the debris or even an animal will be a lot safer than trying to make a sharp turn. Remember no large steering wheel adjustments, ever, at highway speeds. Yes, I know that I already mentioned that. It is that important.

STAYING IN THE CENTER OF THE LANE

After a while you will be able to do this pretty much without conscious thought. Briefly look at the road surface about four or five car lengths ahead. Place yourself slightly to the left of the center of your lane. In the average vehicle, your eyes will be about 16 to 24 inches left of the center of your vehicle. Most roadway lanes are 12 feet wide while the average passenger vehicle won't be wider than six feet. Some in town lanes may be only ten feet wide. This gives you about two to three feet on either side of your vehicle. Once you place yourself just a little left of center of the lane, briefly look in each side view mirror using the lane marking to see if you are centered. With a little practice, you will master this small part of driving without much conscious thought.

YOU DRIVE WHERE YOU LOOK

I once followed behind a friend for about 200 miles while going on a trip. I could tell whenever he was talking to the passenger in the front seat. When he spoke, he would turn his head towards the passenger. When he did so, he would also turn the wheel enough to move the vehicle a few feet to the right. Then he would redirect his attention to the front and return to the center of the lane. He did this for most of the trip.

When a driver looks away from the roadway, for whatever reason, there is a tendency to turn the wheel, ever so slightly, in the same direction as the driver is looking. This happens at accident scenes, when an emergency vehicle is along the roadway. Passing drivers will look over at the accident and their vehicle will drift in that direction. It can happen in just about any other situation where the driver's attention is focused off road. Sometimes a passing driver will drive into a person standing behind a disabled vehicle or right into the accident scene because of this tendency.

Remember to stay in your lane when looking off to the side, for whatever the reason. Remain focused on your driving.

Chapter 4

MAINTAINING CONTROL OF YOUR VEHICLE

MAINTAINING TRACTION, the grip of the tires on the road, is the key for maintaining control of your vehicle. Your tire's footprint, the part contacting the roadway, is small. The average tire's footprint is about the size of an average adult's hand. Even with four tires, that is still a pretty small grip on the road. You need to maintain this grip. Many factors affect this delicate connection. You can control some of these but you will need to understand those you cannot control and make allowances for them. That is the subject of this chapter. To maintain control of your vehicle you must maintain traction. Otherwise you are simply traveling as a passenger in a multiple-ton, unguided missile.

TIRES

You need to have the best tires, in the best condition, maintained at the proper pressure and correctly balanced. They should be the same size, brand and type. Do not mix bias-ply tires with radial tires. Badly worn tires have less traction. Don't ever skimp on tires because of cost. They are too important. You can learn a lot about what type of tires are best for your driving conditions by looking at the manufacturers' websites. Generally, wider tires are good for traction and handling on dry roads. You will see these on sporty vehicles. Wide tires are not so good for rain or snow however. In these conditions, a narrower tire with deep rain grooves will give better traction. For most of us, a combination tire works the best for the average road conditions we might expect. You will find a sticker on the driver's door jamb listing the manufacturer's recommended sizes and tire pressure for that vehicle. However, there is no recommendation included for what type of tire you should use. This will depend on the type of weather and driving you expect to encounter. There are many choices in each size. Do your homework when selecting tires. They are a critical component for maintaining control of your vehicle.

ROAD SURFACES

Concrete

Clean, dry concrete provides good traction. Concrete roadways will have seams running both parallel, and perpendicular, to your direction of travel. Usually the parallel seams are on each side of the lanes. Sometimes the seams in the concrete don't follow the lanes. This can occur in construction areas or after a roadway has been rerouted. Driving on a seam can slightly pull the vehicle in the direction of the seam rather than the marked lane. If the lane markings are faded, you need to pay extra attention to staying in your lane.

Blacktop

Clean, dry blacktop also provides good traction. It is quieter than concrete and, absent repairs, has no seams. However, it is a bit darker at night. There are different types of blacktop. Some look very smooth while others appear to have some gravel or small stones embedded in them.

Gravel

Gravel causes a loss of traction. It isn't a solid surface. Loose gravel will get between the tires and the surface underneath causing the tires to sort of float along the roadway. Have you ever ridden a bicycle on a gravel roadway? Remember how the tires would skid when trying to brake or turn? Sometimes you will encounter patches of gravel and/or soil which has washed onto a concrete or blacktop road. Turning or braking while on gravel will risk loss of traction. If driving on a gravel roadway, reduce your speed to where you can maintain control. Rural gravel roadways are a good place to practice braking and turning to learn how your vehicle will respond. Be sure to do so when it is safe – no other traffic – and at slow speeds.

Shoulders

Oftentimes the shoulder of the road surface will be of a different surface than the roadway. Occasionally it will be just dirt. The tires on the shoulder will have less traction than the tires still on the roadway. If you need to pull onto the shoulder, slow down before driving onto it. Try not to brake hard while your tires are on different surfaces. Brake softly and there will be no problem. If you brake hard, electronic programs controlling the wheels (ABS and Vehicle Stability) should prevent a skid but your stopping distance will be longer than on a solid surface. If your vehicle doesn't have electronic assistance programs, and you brake hard, you will risk a skid, possibly pulling you back into the traffic lane. All newer vehicles should have some type of electronic assist system. Some will have more features than others. Familiarize yourself with your vehicle's electronic assist systems before driving.

Washboard

Washboard is a description of a road surface that is occasionally found on country roads that have been recently graded. It will be a gravel or dirt road. The road surface will have small, two to four-inch-high hills, as wide as the roadway, running sort of perpendicular to the roadway direction. You will quickly learn that travel will be restricted to very slow speeds. Going more than a few miles an hour will make the vehicle rattle and shake. The tires will bounce unless travel is slow, perhaps five or six miles an hour. As you can imagine, a bouncing tire will have limited traction.

Road Construction

You will encounter road construction on all manner of roadways. Roadways need continual maintenance whether it is to fix potholes, sweep debris, repaint lane markings or add new lanes. You may see signs indicating uneven lanes. This occurs when one lane is being resurfaced or a new lane is being added. Usually you won't be able to change lanes because barriers will guide you to stay in your lane. Sometimes you will need to cross a lane that is on a lower level, to exit, for example. Be extra careful as the drop will be four inches or so. You should get across these uneven surfaces as quickly as possible. You don't want the tires to straddle the uneven surface. Also, it is a good idea to hold the steering wheel a bit tighter than normal during the transition.

Extra attention is required where the roadway lane markings do not follow the lane barriers erected for the construction. When you become somewhat comfortable with driving, your subconscious will take over the more mundane actions of driving. Staying in your lane is one of them. Staying in your lane will not require conscious and constant attention as it did when you first began driving. Your subconscious will help to keep you in your lane. The problem can arise when your subconscious is following the lane markings but the construction barriers are not. The barriers will cross lane markings. Be sure to follow the barriers, not the lane markings.

In construction zones, there will be temporary signs with lower speed limits. Some drivers will ignore these. Don't let other drivers control your speed. Pay extra attention when in construction zones, both for your safety and that of the workers on the roadway. Follow the speed limits and look for workers directing traffic. In addition to being safer, you may also avoid a fine which might be imposed for speeding in a construction zone.

ROAD DESIGN

Banked

Banking means that the road surface in a turn will be on an angle rather than level. In a left turn, the left side of the roadway will be lower than the right. Conversely, in a right turn the right side of the roadway will be lower than the left. A banked roadway is common on limited access highways and freeways. Banking makes higher speeds safer in turns as the vehicle stays more level with the roadway rather than leaning to the outside of the turn. Staying level means better traction.

Crowned

The surface of a crowned roadway is highest in the middle of the roadway, sloping downward to both sides of the roadway This is common on rural, two lane roadways. Oftentimes, in turns, the roadway surface will remain crowned rather than banked. This can present a problem. Weight shifting and inertia will occur. Making a left turn on a crowned roadway means the vehicle will be "leaning" away from the turn, rather than into it. This is not a good thing. Making a right turn on a crowned roadway is safer than making a left turn at the same speed. The right turning vehicle will lean into the turn. The vehicle stays more level with the road surface.

41

Staying level means better traction. Making a left turn where the roadway is crowned requires a lower speed than a right turn.

Flat

Some roadways appear flat or almost flat. These are found in towns and cities. Most will be slightly crowned to allow water to drain to the sides of the roadway. As speeds are reduced in towns and cities, the flat surface should present no problems.

Bridges

Oftentimes a bridge will have a different surface than the roadway approaching it. Some will have metal grating rather than concrete or blacktop. This helps with drainage but the metal grating provides less traction than a solid surface roadway. Sometimes the bridge road surface will be in poorer condition than the roadway approaching it. Moisture on the road surface of a bridge will freeze sooner and stay frozen longer than on the surrounding roadways. Avoid hard braking or sudden acceleration. If possible, stay in the same lane. This will minimize any surprises due to inconsistent traction. The road surface of a highway overpass may also freeze sooner and stay frozen longer than the surrounding roadway.

PHYSICAL DEFECTS IN THE ROAD SURFACE

Bumps

Sometimes you will see a sign that says "Bump". Bumps can cause loss of traction, if only for a split second. Slow down a bit and try not to brake or turn while the vehicle is recovering from the bump. If braking is going to be necessary, try to complete it before hitting the bump.

Dips

A dip is a low spot in the roadway. You can usually spot these from a distance. You will see a darker spot in the roadway caused by oil dripping off the underside of previous vehicles as they bottomed out in the dip. The dark spot will be a couple of feet wide and perhaps as long as ten or twelve feet. It looks more like a large smudge rather than a clearly defined spot. Sometimes there will also be grooves in the roadway in the direction of travel. These are caused by trailer hitches and the undercarriage of vehicles that took the dip too fast and dug into the road surface. As the grooves indicate, it will be necessary to reduce your speed to cross the dip comfortably.

- **Large dips** – When encountering one of these, you will usually see a sign that says "Do not enter when flooded". These dips are where a wash crosses the roadway. Heed the signs – do not cross when there is water flowing. The water can be as deep as three or four feet and be fast moving. You will never make it across. Even depths of less than a foot can cause the vehicle to move sideways off the road surface. Walking through fast moving water only a few inches deep can be a challenge. Getting stuck in one of these can be dangerous. When these washes are dry slow down a bit so you don't bottom out.

Potholes

Potholes are holes in the road surface, usually caused by freezing temperature and moisture. Some may be only a few inches deep and maybe a foot across. Others will be wider and a lot deeper. Driving into a deep pothole can cause damage to tires as well as the suspension of your vehicle. Sometimes potholes hide during rain. The rain fills the potholes and it just looks like a wet spot. Potholes are usually somewhat round. If you see a round spot that looks different than the surrounding surface when it is raining it may be a pothole. Potholes don't usually appear alone. They like the company of other potholes. If the roadway is in generally poor condition and you have seen other potholes, that odd, round wet spot may be another pothole. Modern tires can take a lot of punishment but you should avoid these if possible. Usually you can go around or straddle these without changing lanes.

Don't change lanes unless there is room to do so safely. Driving across a pothole is less risky than hitting another vehicle.

Grooves

Sometimes you will see a pair of grooves in the roadway that extend for a long distance, perhaps miles. The grooves are each a little wider than a tire and a vehicle's width apart. These grooves are caused by metal studded snow tires. Once your tires are in the grooves, they will tend to follow them. Hold the steering wheel a little tighter than normal when exiting the grooves.

ENVIRONMENTAL FACTORS

The weather can cause traction problems. Sometimes you will need to avoid driving altogether as weather can make it impossible to drive safely.

Rain

Any moisture will decrease traction to some degree. Rain can eliminate traction altogether by something called hydroplaning. This occurs when a layer of water prevents contact between the tires and the road surface. When hydroplaning occurs, you have lost all control of the vehicle. Think of water skiing or wake-boarding. Once the ski or board gets up enough speed, it skims over the surface of the water. It doesn't sink into the water unless it is going too slowly. The same thing will happen to a vehicle driving too fast for conditions. Hydroplaning can occur with perfect tires and a perfect road surface, if there is a film of water on the road. Under-inflated tires can increase the chance of hydroplaning. It can occur at speeds as low as 30 miles an hour if there is a lot of water. Some tires are better than others in the rain. A good rain tire will be narrow and have some deep straight grooves. However, a narrow tire isn't the best for traction on a clean dry road. A wider tire will grip the road better on a dry road but will tend to hydroplane sooner than a narrow one. A bald tire will hydroplane at a lower speed than a tire in good condition. When selecting tires, consideration needs to be given for the type of weather conditions expected. When driving on a wet road, check the rear-view mirror, looking for the trace of your tires. If you can clearly see the road surface in the tire tracks, for a second or so, your traction is still pretty good. Still not as good as on a dry roadway though. Something else to remember when driving in rain. Never use cruise control. If you start to hydroplane, cruise control will make it worse. It will increase the tire rotation speed, pretty much guaranteeing a total loss of control. Don't use cruise control on snowy roadways either for the same reason.

Puddles

Sometimes you will see water accumulate on the right side of the right lane because of rain runoff. Your right tires will enter the water while the left ones won't. As you might imagine, there will be unequal traction. You don't want to be braking or turning when encountering these puddles. If you enter fast enough, the right tires might even hydroplane. Additionally, as the water is splashed upwards into the right tire wheel wells, it will act as a brake on the right side, tending to pull the vehicle to the right. Slow down before entering. If possible, avoid these by staying out of the right lane. If enough water gets sprayed up into the engine compartment your vehicle might even stall. These puddles are often found in underpasses and in low spots during a heavy rain. Good reason to not drive in these conditions.

Oil in/on the roadway

When it first rains, oil from the roadway will surface and float on top of the water. Until it washes away, the road surface will be more slick than it would be from just the water. A little extra caution is warranted.

Snow

Snow can also play havoc with traction. Wet snow can fill the grooves in the tires. Then traction will be equivalent to driving on bald tires. Some tires are better than others at shedding snow. Even dry, blowing snow can affect traction. A lower speed is called for when driving in snow. Driving in an inch or two should be fine if speed is reasonable. Any more than a couple of inches can cause serious traction problems. Even though you have good tires and are driving slowly, there will always be people out there who will not reduce their speed. It is not a good idea to be driving in snow until the roads are cleared and/or sanded. Four-wheel drive vehicles have an advantage in snowy conditions but as a new driver, avoid driving until the roads are plowed and sanded.

Ice

It is impossible to drive safely on ice. There is no traction. Even with studded tires, it is impossible to maintain good traction. Studded tires give some traction if speed is slow. But there is a tradeoff. It has been my experience that studs can cause skidding if the studs strike the road surface. This occurs when there are wet spots interspersed with ice due to salting, sanding or sunlight. They also aren't much good if there is a combination of snow and snow-covered ice. Icy roadways are no place for inexperienced drivers. Icy roads are no place for most drivers. Leave the icy roads for the plows and sanders.

Some localities will use a salt and sand mixture for snowy or icy roads. Other localities will use just sand. Even after the snow or ice has melted, the sand can interfere with traction.

Black Ice

Black ice is a term for ice that is particularly hard to spot. It refers to a thin coating of ice which is virtually transparent. You will see the roadway surface below. It will look like a dark, wet spot. It can occur in patches on otherwise dry or clean road surfaces. There is no traction when crossing these spots. The best you can do is avoid braking and turning until past the ice. If black ice occurs on a turn or a hill, loss of control will occur. Likely locations for black ice will be shady spots along an otherwise sunny roadway. It can also appear where water has run onto the roadway from a hillside. If the weather is somewhere around freezing, those "wet" spots may be black ice. Early morning, after a colder night can produce these. Avoid this risk by not driving until roadways have been cleared and the sun, hopefully, will have melted the icy spots.

Temperature

When the temperature is or has been right around freezing there can be icy spots. Bridges and raised roadway surfaces cool sooner and stay cold longer than the surrounding roadway. This means that there may be ice on a bridge or raised roadway even though the surrounding roadways are clear. Air temperature can also affect road conditions as altitude increases. Air temperature will drop as altitude increases. If you are driving uphill on a wet roadway and the temperature is approaching freezing, the roadway up ahead will be colder. Ice may well be on the roadway.

I once responded to an accident in just such a situation. It was shortly after sunrise and the temperature was near freezing. A light rain had just begun. The vehicle had come up a long, wet hill. As the roadway leveled off at the top, it turned slightly to the left. The roadway was covered with black ice beginning at the crest for about 200 feet or so. There was a guardrail on the right shoulder. When the vehicle drove onto the black ice, the driver lost control. The vehicle continued straight into the guardrail, sliding along for perhaps 100 feet or so. A bus, which later crashed on another patch of black ice, skidded sideways but made it through the turn. While trying to set out flares, I had to dive over the guardrail twice to avoid being struck. Within a short time, twelve other vehicles coming up the hill also struck the guardrail. A few drivers managed to make the gentle turn. They were driving more slowly. They skidded around a bit but managed to stay on the roadway. The others could have remained on the roadway if they thought about the temperature, the increasing altitude and the wet road surface. They should have expected the possibility of ice and driven accordingly. Fortunately, there were no serious injuries. The black ice remained for an hour or so until the sun and rising temperatures melted it.

Wind

Wind will affect control of a vehicle. Wind of a few miles an hour will present no problems. High winds, on the other hand, can overturn trucks and other large vehicles and push smaller vehicles around. Couple high wind with a slippery road surface, as in a rainstorm, and you have control problems. Tractor-trailer drivers will pull off the roadway when winds are too severe. You should also. Even small vehicles, because they tend to be light, can get pushed off the roadway, or worse, into oncoming traffic by a combination of high wind and wet roads. Wind also creates visibility problems when it blows sand and dirt across roadways. It also deposits sand and soil onto the roadway. All the traction issues discussed so far can be exacerbated by high winds. Pay attention to weather advisories and just don't drive when weather conditions add to the dangers of driving.

TURBULENCE

Air turbulence caused by other traffic can affect control of your vehicle. Have you ever stood near a roadway when a tractor-trailer passed by at highway speeds? As the cab passes, it pushes air out of and around the truck's path. Then as the trailer passes, the air returns behind the trailer. You can hear a sort of whooshing sound as papers and dust are sucked behind the trailer. This happens with all vehicles but is more noticeable with larger trucks. When a tractor-trailer or other large vehicle passes you in the same direction, you might notice a slight buffeting of your vehicle as it passes. It will feel as if a wind gust hit the side of your vehicle. Normally this doesn't pose a problem. However, this turbulence can cause a real problem under certain conditions.

Imagine that you are driving on a two-lane roadway, one lane each way separated by a double line. A larger vehicle is traveling in the opposite direction. The turbulence from that vehicle will be much greater than if you were traveling in the same direction. Now suppose the roadway is wet. What effect will the turbulence have on your vehicle? Will it cause you to lose control? The risk will be greater as you will have less traction on a wet road than you would on a dry one. I have seen smaller vehicles get pulled across half a lane, towards the oncoming lane, when it was raining. I don't know how many accidents might be caused by this air turbulence, but as vehicles get smaller while trucks remain the same size, I am willing to bet that there will be an increase. So, what can you do about it? It is like everything else you learn about driving. Once you realize what the problems are, you can minimize or eliminate them. It is the unknown that will get you into trouble. In this case, stay as far away as you can from the other vehicle. Move to the extreme edge of your lane to increase the distance between yourself and oncoming traffic. If the roadway is wet, drive more slowly. Avoid fast traffic when the weather is bad. Don't drive on two lane roadways if you have a choice. Head on traffic is always more deadly than one way traffic.

VEHICLE DYNAMICS

We have talked about factors that can affect traction and, as a result, your ability to control your vehicle. Now let's talk about the laws of physics as applied to a vehicle's movements and how they also affect your ability to maintain control. Some of the following information, especially the formulas, may seem complicated. It isn't necessary to remember all the specifics. There won't be a test on formulas. But you will get an appreciation for how the laws of physics can assist, or impair, your driving.

Inertia

Newton's First Law of Motion applies anytime you are in a moving vehicle. An object at rest tends to stay at rest whereas an object in motion tends to stay in motion. Vehicles in motion, unless acted upon by an outside force, will tend to stay in motion. Look at that, you are already using something you learned in junior high school. This tendency of the vehicle to resist the change in motion is called inertia. This means that your vehicle wants to travel in a straight line and at the same speed. Well your vehicle doesn't "want" anything but it seems to make sense to explain it this way. Some of the factors that affect inertia include friction of the tires with the road surface, air resistance, and gravity. These might slow you down a bit but are of minor concern for normal driving situations. Accelerating, turning, and braking are factors that you control. They are the tools that you will use to control inertia. It is the traction of the tires to the roadway that allows you to do so.

Momentum

Momentum can be calculated by multiplying mass times velocity. The weight of your vehicle times the speed of your vehicle. A moving vehicle will have a large momentum if it has large mass as well as high speed. Conversely, a lighter vehicle, traveling at a slower speed will have, proportionally, a lower momentum. If two vehicles are traveling at the same speed, the vehicle with the greater mass will have a higher momentum. A 2000-pound vehicle traveling at 25mph has 50,000 foot pounds of energy (fpe), 25(the speed) times 2000 (the weight).

If you double the speed of the 2000-pound vehicle to 50 mph, you have 100,000 fpe. The greater the momentum, the greater the forces acting on your vehicle to resist change of direction. Why is this important for you to know? Well, the faster you drive, the greater the tendency of your vehicle to continue in a straight line. A larger momentum isn't necessarily a bad thing, as we will see when selecting a safer vehicle. But for maintaining traction, momentum does cause issues. The faster you drive the more difficult it becomes to maintain traction when turning, braking or accelerating.

Kinetic Energy

Kinetic energy of an object is the energy it possesses due to its motion. To get a vehicle up to speed takes kinetic energy. It is the work needed to accelerate a vehicle of a given weight from rest to a given speed. The same amount of energy will be needed to decelerate the vehicle to a stop. For driving, this is the more relevant factor. The formula for kinetic energy is one half the mass times the velocity squared. Let's use the same vehicle weight and speed as we used in the momentum formula – a 2000-pound vehicle traveling at 25 mph. One half the weight (1000 pounds) times the speed squared (625) gives us 625,000 Joules, the standard unit of measurement for kinetic energy. Now let's double the speed. Half the weight (1000) times the speed of 50 mph squared (2,500) gives us 2,500,000 Joules. Doubling the speed quadruples the kinetic energy. Now, why is this important for you to understand? By doubling your speed from 25 mph to 50 mph it will take four times the kinetic energy to stop your vehicle. This means it will take four times the braking distance to stop your vehicle at 50 mph as it will at 25 mph. Your braking distance multiplies when your speed doubles. Whatever your safe stopping distance is at a given speed, if you double it, you will need four times the distance for the braking portion of your stopping distance.

Weight Shifting

Weight shifting means that weight from one tire shifts to another due to various movements of the vehicle. When a vehicle is designed, the engineers determine the optimum weight distribution for each axle. Tire sizes are then selected for their proper weight handling abilities. Weight shifting occurs continually when driving, unless you are traveling on a flat, straight road at a constant speed. It is caused by accelerating, braking, turning and the attitude of the vehicle. Vehicles are designed to allow for changes in weight shifting and still provide a safe driving experience. It is not something that you need to continually monitor. It is when you over drive a vehicle's handling abilities, that weight shifting becomes a problem. Let's look at how your vehicle's weight shifts in response to various driving conditions.

- **Acceleration** – When accelerating, the front of the car will rise a slight bit putting more weight on the rear tires. A cushy riding vehicle will do so more than a sportier model.

- **Braking** – When braking, inertia will cause some weight shifting from the rear tires to the front tires. You can see this happen. Watch when another vehicle brakes. You will see the front of the car dip down. Some vehicles will dip more than others. When braking in a curve, weight shifting creates uneven traction. Making a left turn will cause some weight to shift to the right side of the vehicle, placing more weight on the right tires. Making a right turn will cause weight shifting to the left.

- **Uphill** – Traveling uphill will shift weight to the rear tires.

57

- **Downhill** – Traveling downhill will shift weight to the front tires.

- **Curves** – Weight will shift to the outside of the curve. A turn to the left causes a weight shift to the right tires. A turn to the right causes a weight shift to the left.

Combine any two or more weight shifting actions and you will have a combination of weight shifting among the tires.

SKIDS

In the Vehicle Dynamics section, we discussed inertia, momentum, kinetic energy and weight shifting. Now let's see how these dynamics affect traction.

Loss of traction of one or more tires will result in a skid. It may be a split-second skid of one tire and barely noticeable. Or it may be a heart stopping, all wheel, 360-degree skid on ice or snow. When you are in a skid, you have lost control of your vehicle.

If your vehicle has one of the vehicle stability control systems (VSC), it will assist in regaining control by applying braking to the various wheels. Some VSC systems will also reduce power to assist with control. Current VSC will not turn the steering wheel for you. As this manual is being written, some electronic control systems are being created to take control of the steering as well. This is a good example of why it is critical for you to know what electronic systems are on your vehicle.

Let's suppose you enter a left, downhill turn too fast. You step hard on the brake pedal and turn the steering wheel to the left. Inertia, momentum, kinetic energy and weight shifting are all involved, but how? Inertia is trying to keep the vehicle on a straight course. Momentum from going too fast will fight the attempt to slow down. Kinetic energy will be too great for the vehicle to slow as quickly as needed. Some weight shifts from the left rear to the right front. A lesser amount shifts from the right rear to the front. The rear of the vehicle lifts. The front dives down and leans to the right. There is inadequate traction on the rear tires. Inertia "wants" the vehicle to continue straight. The front tires, with additional weight, have adequate traction. The front of the vehicle turns to the left. The rear tires have less weight bearing down on the roadway. They cannot maintain traction. Momentum overcomes the inadequate traction of the rear tires and causes the rear of the vehicle to swing around to the right. Not good. The right side of the vehicle is facing the direction of travel. See the following diagram.

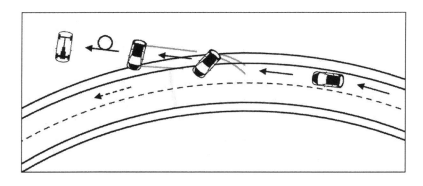

The vehicle skids sideways on the hard road surface. Weight has been shifting to the right-side tires but there is still enough weight on the left tires for the vehicle to remain upright. The vehicle skids across the shoulder and into a soft, grassy surface. What happens next? The tires no longer skid. They dig into the soft soil and all weight shifts to the right side. As the tires dig in, skidding stops. Momentum and inertia cause the vehicle to roll over. Notice that this problem is the result of too much speed. You now know what happened and why. All you need to remember is that too much speed caused this problem. All vehicles are designed to handle inertia, momentum, kinetic energy and weight shifting. Some better than others. But they all have their limits. Too much speed will cause you to exceed the ability of your vehicle to maintain traction. Then the laws of physics will determine where your vehicle will go regardless of your intentions.

Note regarding all diagrams. A solid line depicts where the car has travelled. A dotted line indicates where the driver intended to go.

Types of skids

There are three causes of driver induced skids: over accelerating, over braking and over cornering. These situations are mostly caused by too much speed. Weather and road conditions can make skidding more likely but they are not the causes of skids. They are factors which you must allow for. You need to tailor your driving to the road and environmental factors we discussed earlier.

- **Accelerating skids** – also known as power skids. This is caused by applying too much power too quickly. Doing so causes the drive wheels to spin faster than the vehicle can accelerate. Traction will be lost and the vehicle may well spin one way or the other. Most production vehicles won't have enough power to cause this type of skid from a standing start when on a level, dry road surface. However, most vehicles can be put into a power skid on a snowy or even a wet surface. Experienced race car drivers will use skidding sideways, known as drifting, as a method of making turns at high speeds. This is not for you. Public roadways are no place for drifting. Race cars are designed to allow for this. Passenger vehicles are designed to help avoid drifting skids.

To get out of an acceleration skid, ease your foot off the accelerator and turn the steering wheel in the direction of the skid. If the back end of your vehicle is skidding to the left, turn the wheel to the left. If it is skidding to the right, turn the wheel to the right. On a snowy or wet road, once the front tires have regained traction, gingerly apply the accelerator or brakes as needed. If the roadway is dry, corrections using the accelerator and brakes can be done more quickly. If you are lucky enough to be able to practice this maneuver on a training track or other safe place, it will be a great opportunity to learn the "feel" of your vehicle – how it responds to correcting a skid.

- **Braking skids** – These are caused by applying too much brake pedal for the speed you are traveling. You are asking the tires to maintain traction beyond their ability to do so. Maximum traction occurs just before a skid. A rolling tire has better traction than one that is skidding. There are three types of braking skids: front-wheel, rear-wheel and all-wheel. In a front-wheel skid, the vehicle will travel in a straight line. There will be no steering control. In a rear-wheel skid, the rear of the vehicle will swing around either to the right or the left. In an all-wheel skid, the vehicle will spin in either direction, turning 360 degrees, one or more times. This can easily occur on snow if braking too hard. It is pretty much guaranteed to occur on ice. When in a skid you needn't think about what wheels are skidding. You will react depending on what the vehicle is doing.

ABS is an abbreviation for an electronic Anti-Lock Braking System found on most, if not all, currently manufactured passenger vehicles. Unless you are driving a very old vehicle, it will be on yours. ABS will prevent, or at least correct, most of these skids if it is activated. To activate it, you must brake hard and keep hard pedal pressure until the emergency is over. Soft pedal pressure will not activate it. When activated, you will feel a pulsating in the brake pedal and a loud, possibly very loud, grating or groaning sound coming from under the passenger compartment. This tells you it is working. ABS will apply and release the brakes to each wheel many times a second which will help prevent loss of traction. When ABS first came out, vehicle manufacturers didn't provide enough information to new car owners about what to expect when ABS is engaged. Drivers would automatically release brake pressure when the brake pulsing and noise occurred. Serious accidents resulted, even among experienced, professional drivers. Now that you know what will happen, don't be frightened by the pulsing and the noise. Expect it and be happy your electronic systems are working to make the best possible adjustments to regain control. Maintain hard pedal pressure until the emergency is over.

To get out of a braking skid when trying to stop in a straight line, simply step hard on the brake pedal. This will force ABS to engage. You will stop as quickly as possible, given the road conditions. The ABS will prevent the wheels from locking up. Keep the steering wheel in a forward direction.

When skidding in a turn, steer in the direction of the skid. If the rear of your vehicle is coming around to the right, while you are trying to go left, steer to the right. This may seem counter intuitive as the skid isn't in the direction you want to go. But until the rear wheels are tracking the front wheels, the skid will continue. Once the rear wheels are tracking the front wheels return the steering to the direction desired. Likewise, if you are making a right turn and the rear comes around to the left, steer to the left.

There are some older vehicles and commercial trucks which do not have either ABS or some type of stability control. The techniques for using the brakes in these vehicles are different than those for electronically assisted vehicles. In these vehicles, you do not hold heavy brake pressure when in a skid. The brakes are released until steering control is regained, Then the brake pedal is "pumped". The object is to apply brakes up to, but not beyond, lockup of the wheels. The pedal is released and pressed rapidly until control is regained. As you can imagine this is not nearly as effective as ABS. Make sure that any vehicle you drive has ABS.

- **Cornering skids** – This type of skid occurs when you enter a turn too fast.

To get out of a cornering skid, ease off the gas and steer in the direction of the skid. If you skid while making a right turn, the rear of the vehicle will slide around to the left. You would need to steer to the left. Once the rear tires again track the front, return the steering wheel to the direction intended. If making a left turn, the rear of the vehicle will swing around to the right. Steer to the right until the rear tires track the front before returning the steering to the left. Apply power softly to avoid another skid. As you can imagine, you might have very little room on the roadway to make this maneuver before running out of road surface. It needs to be made as quickly as possible along with the return of the wheel to the intended direction. Caution is needed here. Do not over correct the steering wheel in either direction. You should have a tight grip on the wheel and make small wheel adjustments, especially when returning the steering to the intended direction. Too much input to the wheel will result in a skid in the opposite direction. This is called over-correcting and has been the cause of many serious accidents. Remember, always small steering wheel adjustments at highway speeds. Yep, I'm going to keep repeating that until it is imprinted into your subconscious.

Correcting a cornering skid is a technique that should be practiced in a professional setting or at least using a go-cart track rather than learned during a life-threatening situation on the public road. With a few practice skids, it can easily be learned. You will then react automatically before you have even thought about it.

Understeer and Oversteer

Understeer means a vehicle will continue in a straight line if you enter a turn beyond the capability of the vehicle to maintain traction with all four tires. The front tires lose traction and you lose the ability to turn the vehicle.

Oversteer means a vehicle will lose rear wheel traction when entering a turn too fast. The result is a rear wheel skid.

Passenger cars are designed to have slight understeer. Continuing straight when entering a turn too fast is generally safer than losing traction to the rear tires, skidding sideways and possibly rolling over. Race cars are designed to oversteer. This allows the driver to "drift" through a turn. Drifting through a turn on a race track, under controlled conditions, by experienced drivers, makes racing exciting but it has no place in day-to-day driving.

STEERING

At low speeds, as in making a right angle turn in an intersection, you will turn the steering wheel as much as 180 degrees, maybe more. You will be making a sharp turn in a limited space. You need to make a large steering wheel adjustment to make the turn. You can do so safely if your speed is low, just a few miles per hour. As speed increases, make progressively smaller adjustments. You will have much more distance to complete a lane change or negotiate a curve. At highway speeds, moving the steering wheel an inch or two is all that is needed. Large wheel adjustments are not only unnecessary, they are extremely dangerous. A large wheel adjustment at highway speed will cause a rear-wheel skid with a possibility of a rollover.

Turns

Remember the discussion about kinetic energy when braking? When you double your speed, your braking distance quadruples. Something similar happens when making a turn. Doubling your speed in a turn quadruples the pounds of sideways force pushing your vehicle from its intended path. This force is measured in G s. In addition, a tight turn will exert more G force than a mild turn. The tighter the turn, the lower the speed necessary to successfully negotiate it. Some older freeway off-ramps even have turns with a diminishing curve – the curve gets tighter as you approach the end. Pay close attention to the yellow warning signs preceding off ramps. They are there because highway engineers have determined a safe exit speed. But remember, this is for optimum driving conditions. You still may need a much lower speed in inclement weather.

SPEED

Your speed should always be what is referred to as "reasonable and prudent". Increasing speed increases all factors which can decrease traction. Drive at the speed where you have maximum traction, given the road conditions and the environment. This takes experience. Each vehicle will handle differently, whether on a dry road surface or one with water, snow or other factor that reduces traction.

You should not drive the posted speed limit if there is rain, snow, ice, fog, heavy traffic or any other factor that reduces your ability to maximize control of your vehicle. It may be reasonable and prudent to drive 10 mph even though the posted limit is 35. Fog, rain or snow can all require a lower speed. On the other hand, you need to keep up with traffic, rather than become an impediment to it. Driving the speed limit in the left lane of a super highway when all other traffic in that lane is traveling ten miles over the limit is not safe. Move into a slower lane. Sometimes the speed limits seem too low and at other times, too high. A speed that is safe during the day in fair weather won't be near as safe in the rain or at night.

In my experience, if traffic is light, the weather is clear, and the road is in good condition, there will be plenty of drivers exceeding the posted limit. I am not suggesting that you ignore speed limit signs, but if all traffic is moving at a few miles over the limit, it is safer to move with traffic than to cause it to back up behind you. I would take safety over blindly following speed signs. Sometimes you will need to drive much slower than the posted limit and sometimes it is safer to go slightly over it. If traffic is constantly building up behind you and then passing you, increase your speed, or move into a slower lane.

Cruise Control

As a novice driver you should not be using cruise control at all. It will create problems for you. It will maintain a constant speed which can cause too much speed when driving downhill and in turns. It is especially troublesome when driving both downhill and in a turn. I only use it when on a long drive on a relatively straight and level roadway. You should do likewise, but only when you become a skilled driver. Cruise control can create a very serious problem when the road is wet. It will increase the speed of the tires' rotation, possibly turning what might have been a temporary hydroplane into a total loss of steering control.

Maintaining a safe distance

Common advice is to use the "Two Second Rule" to maintain a safe distance between your vehicle and the one in front. It is an easy way to maintain a safe space. It doesn't require the ability to judge distance – just to count seconds. Simply count the seconds it takes you to reach the same spot in the road as the vehicle in front. As it passes a lane seam, a traffic sign or a shadow, count "one thousand one - one thousand two". If you haven't reached the same spot before reaching "two", you

70

are maintaining a reasonably safe distance. If you reach it before the two seconds are up, allow more room. I use three seconds and suggest you do likewise. If the traffic is light on a highway, I will even use five seconds. That gives plenty of room to avoid any hazards that might appear in your path.

Sometimes it will be hard to maintain even a two-second space as traffic will continually move into the space you left. This will occur in heavy traffic that isn't quite heavy enough to cause a traffic jam. Don't give up, just keep adjusting as best you can. Even if other drivers keep cutting in front, it will only delay your trip by a few seconds or minutes. A small price to pay for remaining safe. Practice counting seconds at home if you don't feel comfortable that your timing is accurate.

BRAKING

We talked about braking when skidding, and using the anti-lock braking system. In other than emergency situations, braking will not involve the ABS system. You will remain in control of how and when to brake. The goal is to always brake smoothly. When braking is necessary for a turn, brake ahead of the turn. The ideal speed to enter a turn is one in which no additional braking is necessary to reduce your speed during the turn. Accelerating slightly in a curve gives better control.

In a downhill turn, you would not accelerate until the turn is completed. You might even have to brake for most of the turn just to maintain a safe speed.

Testing the ABS System

First, read your operator's manual to learn the electronic vehicle control systems for your vehicle. Then, learn how the vehicle acts when the ABS operates. Select a safe area away from traffic. On a dry, clean road surface. accelerate to 15 mph and step on the brake pedal as you would to slow down normally. The vehicle should slow down and travel straight ahead without any corrections to the steering wheel. It should stop in a straight line. Then try it at 25 mph. The vehicle should again stop in a straight line. Once you have determined that the brakes are operating without any problems, accelerate to 15 mph and "stomp" hard on the brake pedal. Do not remove pedal pressure. If the speed was enough to cause the ABS system to engage, you will hear the loud, growling or grating sound and feel the brake pedal pulsating. You can release the pedal pressure once stopped. Now try it at 25 mph. If the ABS didn't operate at 15 mph, it should have operated at 25. Now that you know what to expect in an emergency, when ABS engages with all that noise and the pulsating brake pedal, it won't be a surprise. ABS works great but it is not a cure all. It helps you to stop in a bad situation. It is better to not get into the bad situation where ABS engages. Hopefully, you will never need it.

Stopping distances – Stopping distances are a combination of three different factors: *perception time* – the time it takes you to recognize the need to brake; *reaction time* – the time it takes to move your foot from the gas pedal to the brake; and *braking distance* – the actual distance it takes the tires to stop the vehicle.

At 30 miles per hour a vehicle travels almost 45 feet per second. At 60 miles per hour, about 90 feet per second. Let's look at that in practical terms. Your state driving manual will have a chart showing approximate stopping distances for an average car, on a level dry road in good condition, assuming good brakes and tires. Some manuals may not address all three factors, leaving out either perception time or reaction time.

- *Perception Time* – The current edition of the commercial driver's license manual for my home state, Idaho, states the perception time for an alert driver is about 1¾ seconds. This is for a driver that is not distracted by talking, looking elsewhere or just daydreaming. She is focused on driving.

- **Reaction Time** – This manual also lists the average reaction time for an alert driver to move her foot from the gas pedal to the brake pedal as ¾ of a second.

- **Braking Distance** – The Idaho non-commercial driver's manual lists a braking distance of 50 feet for a speed of 30 miles an hour for the average car. This is for a dry, level roadway in good condition along with good tires and brakes.

At 30 miles an hour the total distance traveled during the perception and the reaction times would be 2 ½ times 45 feet for a total of 112 ½ feet. Adding the distance of 112 ½ feet for perception and reaction time, plus 50 feet for braking, gives us 162 ½ feet of stopping distance at 30 mph.

Now let's look at the stopping distance for 60 miles an hour. You might assume that the total stopping distance would simply double to 325 feet. It's actually 425 feet. But why? The answer is braking distance quadruples, not doubles, at double the speed. Remember the discussion about kinetic energy? When you double the speed, kinetic energy quadruples. It takes four times as much energy to stop the vehicle at 60 miles per hour than what is required to stop it at 30 miles per hour. The perception and reaction times remain the same so the distance traveled at twice the speed only doubles. However, the braking distance quadruples. Driving at double the speed requires more than double the distance to stop.

Many interstates allow 70 miles per hour. At that speed you will have traveled 262 ½ feet during perception and reaction time. Adding an estimated braking distance of 272 feet means you would need 534 ½ feet to stop. That is almost the length of two football fields. Remember this is under optimal conditions – good weather, level road surface in good condition, good brakes and good, properly inflated tires. Apply the brakes early and smoothly rather than slamming them on with screeching tires and frightened cries from your passengers.

VSC – This is another computer controlled program for helping to prevent skids as well as regaining control. Other names for this type of program include ESC (electronic stability control), ESP (electronic stability program) and DSC (dynamic stability control). Some combine ABS with throttle control to maintain your ability to control steering. The programs do this by tracking the speed of each wheel, throttle position, steering wheel position and lateral acceleration. If the computer senses that you are losing control, or the vehicle is not following its intended path, VSC takes over. Once again, be sure to understand the systems in your vehicle and what they can do. Both ABS and VSC have reduced fatalities. Vehicle manufacturers are continually incorporating additional systems to improve driving safety. Whenever you are about to drive a different vehicle, a rental for example, familiarize yourself with its electronic safety systems before starting.

Down Shifting

Shifting to a lower gear is sometimes preferable to braking when going downhill, especially on a long downgrade. Using a lower gear is easier on the brakes and, more importantly, provides better control of your vehicle. When entering a steep, downhill roadway, shift the transmission to a lower gear. Caution – do not do this at high speeds. Approaching a long downhill grade requires a slower than normal speed to begin with. At the crest of a hill you should be traveling no faster than the speed at which it is reasonable to descend. Shift to one gear lower at the beginning of the down grade. This will use the engine to help slow your speed and reduce the need for hard or constant braking. You may even need to shift to another lower gear to maintain a safe speed without constantly using the brakes. Some vehicles have as many as nine forward gears while others may only have three or four.

Practice using lower gears as part of learning about your vehicle. Do this in a safe location, not in traffic.

Visual Distance

You should always be able to stop within the distance that you can see. Snow, rain, fog, dust and nighttime will limit your view ahead. Do not over drive your visual/stopping distance. Doing so is a gamble with your life.

Chapter 5

COMMON DRIVING SITUATIONS

SHARED LANES

SHARED LANES ARE also called two-way or suicide lanes. You will see them mostly in commercial areas. They are found in the center of the roadway and allow traffic from either direction to use them. There will be one or two lanes on either side. They are marked with a solid yellow line on the outside and a dashed yellow line on the inside. When two vehicles, traveling in opposite directions, enter the shared lane intending to turn left, there can be a problem.

The car traveling south wants to turn east into a store parking lot while the other car, traveling north, wants to turn west into a shopping center lot.

As each wants to turn left after it passes the other vehicle one must give way. But which one will? See the following diagram.

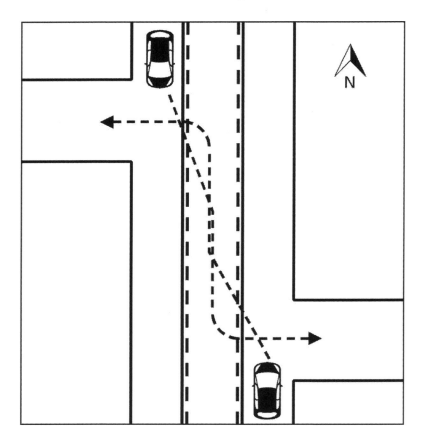

The best way to avoid this problem is to give plenty of notice of your intent to turn left by signaling and slowing down well before entering the lane. Be aware of traffic on your right and those coming from behind in case you need to return to the right traffic lane due to oncoming traffic already in the shared lane.

CALIFORNIA STOP

This is also, known as a California roll. This isn't a stop although it should be. It is a failure to come to a complete stop when required to do so. It occurs mostly when a driver intends to turn right. The driver will slow down just enough to make the turn even though the traffic light or sign requires a stop. Just because you have the right of way doesn't mean you will get it. The California stop is somewhat common at four way stops and certainly when folks are making a right turn at a lighted intersection. Never trust that a driver will come to a complete stop. Don't just proceed because you have the right of way. Make sure it is safe to proceed.

BLUFF STOP

Imagine driving along, approaching a road intersecting from your right. A vehicle is approaching from that roadway at a high rate of speed, so fast that it looks like it couldn't stop even if the driver intended to. You slow down to avoid a possible accident. Most times the driver will brake hard and make the stop but you can't take the chance he will. I call this a bluff stop because it appears that the other driver is attempting to bluff you into giving him the right of way even though he is not entitled to it. Once you have passed the intersecting roadway, if the vehicle pulls in behind you, keep

81

an eye on him. If he crowds you, let him by. It is generally safer to have an unsafe driver in front of you than behind.

MAKING A LEFT TURN INTO A BUSINESS DRIVEWAY

There are two things to remember when making a left turn into a shopping center or similar multi-use business parking lot. First, while stopped, keep your wheels straight ahead until beginning the turn. This will prevent being pushed into the opposing traffic lane if struck from behind. Second, if there is a vehicle turning into the same driveway ahead of you wait until it is at least one vehicle length past the sidewalk before beginning your turn. This will allow you to completely enter the lot in case the driver in front decides to stop just after entering the lot. If you follow the vehicle and it stops just in the entrance you will be broadside to oncoming traffic. Not a good thing.

BLIND SPOTS

Even with properly adjusted mirrors you will have somewhat of a blind spot just off your right rear fender. Just as you don't want a driver in your blind spot, you don't want to be in another's blind spot. When passing another vehicle on the right, pass right through his blind spot. Don't stay there. Be wary of that vehicle suddenly moving into your lane when passing through his blind spot.

As I am writing this section, car manufacturers are continually adding more electronic tools for drivers. I imagine that soon a dashboard screen will display a 360-degree view around your vehicle. This will show all vehicles that are in proximity to yours. There may also be an audible signal indicating any "too close" vehicle. In the meantime, we still must use our mirrors and look over our right shoulder to check the blind spot. Interestingly, there are larger blind spots in our newer vehicles than in the older ones. Front and rear window posts have gotten thicker to better support the roof in a rollover and to hold airbags. Rear view mirrors have gotten larger as well. These may make driving safer but they do make larger blind spots.

TRAFFIC SIGNAL PATTERNS

We will talk about this a bit in the chapter on intersections. Different cities and towns will have their own traffic signal patterns. Some will have lagging left turn signals while others will have leading left turn signals. Some will have smart lights which adjust for traffic flow while other traffic lights will be timed. Some have longer yellow light patterns than others. This means that you cannot let your subconscious control your intersection driving. If you don't know the specific light pattern for the intersection pay extra attention to the timing of the lights.

A family member of mine, living in Coeur d'Alene, Idaho, narrowly avoided a serious intersection accident because of intersection light patterns. He was used to leading left turn signals. Whenever the light turned green he could immediately make a left turn. When he visited in Arizona, he immediately entered an intersection to make a left turn on a green signal. The problem – there was no left turn signal. He was accustomed to turning as soon as there was a green signal. He did not notice that the green light was for through traffic only. Opposing traffic also entered the intersection as they had a green light as well. Fortunately, all vehicles stopped, avoiding a collision.

We talked about your subconscious making driving easier by taking over the more mundane tasks like staying in the center of a lane. However, intersections require our full, conscious attention. This is no time for automatic responses by the subconscious.

STOPPING

When stopping behind another vehicle leave enough room between your vehicle and it to allow for a margin of safety. Stop far enough back so you can see where the tires on the vehicle in front touch the ground.

USING A PILOT VEHICLE

When traveling long distances, and the traffic isn't too heavy, pick out a vehicle to follow. One that is being driven safely. One that is not speeding, not making constant lane changes, not constantly braking. One that stays in the center one or two lanes of a multiple lane highway. This should be a vehicle that doesn't block your vision to the front and one that does not have any cargo that could come loose such as bicycles or cargo containers. By following, you will be able to anticipate any problem that the driver in this "pilot" vehicle sees before you do. If the driver brakes, you can expect to do likewise. This can make a long drive a little bit easier. This is also a great technique when driving at night on an unfamiliar road.

I prefer to pick out a tractor-trailer – lots of lights on the trailer makes it easier to see. These professional drivers, as a group, are among the safest drivers out there. They usually will know the roads as well. Just don't follow too closely. On rural roads or even interstate highways with light traffic, I will stay back ten seconds or more. Having an additional pair of eyes far ahead of you will let you know of all turns, dips and other road changes or hazards well ahead of your getting there.

TRACTOR-TRAILERS

While we are talking about tractor-trailers, lets discuss some common courtesies to extend to those drivers. While you may be driving a vehicle that weighs a few thousand pounds, the tractor-trailer driver may be hauling a total weight of 80,000 pounds or so. This does not include those "over width" vehicles you will occasionally encounter. These vehicles take longer to get up to speed and to slow down. They take a lot more room to turn. They have numerous gears and are shifting almost constantly when in town. They are wider than your vehicle which leaves less side to side clearance in their lane.

All of this makes it a lot tougher to drive a tractor-trailer as safely as you hope they will. How does this impact you? What should you do? When in town, give them extra time and room to make turns. If you are going to pull in front of them on the highway, give them plenty of warning by signaling your intention. When you see one on a downgrade do not pull right in front of them to necessitate the need for them to brake or downshift. Don't pull in front until you are matching or exceeding their speed. Pass for at least four or five vehicle lengths before pulling in front. They will silently thank you for your consideration.

CHOICE OF ROADWAY

If you had a choice between driving on a divided highway with a median and barriers and driving on a two-lane highway divided only by a painted line, which would you choose? You would always choose the safer one, right? The divided highway, even one with only one lane each way will be safer if it is separated by barriers. It will be the safer route, even if the speeds are faster. One-way traffic will always be the safer bet. Head on traffic is extremely dangerous. Take the longer route. A few minutes longer driving is a small price to pay to remain safe.

CHOICE OF LANE

If there are multiple lanes in your direction which should you choose? There are too many variations to list them all here. Besides, you would probably fall asleep before you could read them all. Your goal is to always be in the lane that has the minimum risk of an accident. Let's look at some general guidelines.

In town – You will usually have one or two lanes in each direction. With one lane, there is no choice. Hazards can appear from either the left or the right. But when there are two lanes in your direction and they are separated by a shared lane, the left lane is my choice. This lane provides an out either way, left or right, should some potential hazard appear. In this lane, you avoid the problem of a vehicle parked along the curb suddenly pulling out into the right lane. You also eliminate the risk of a driver or passenger in that vehicle opening a door into the traffic lane.

If there are two lanes in each direction separated only by pavement markings, then generally, my first choice is the right lane. When the roadway veers to the left, oncoming traffic drives towards you until completion of the turn. If an oncoming vehicle comes over the center line, the right most lane will allow you the most time for evasive action. This is especially important when traveling uphill while the roadway curves left. An oncoming vehicle will have a greater tendency to come over the center line if its speed is too high, the roadway is slippery, the driver is distracted or the vehicle is towing a trailer. If this occurs, that vehicle will be forced into the inside lane on your side. The longer the turn continues and the sharper the turn, the greater the risk.

Notice that I addressed only left turns as creating a potential problem. That is because in a right curving roadway, the oncoming traffic isn't driving towards you while making the turn. Although you would be driving towards opposing traffic while in the turn, if your speed is reasonable for the conditions, you won't be a hazard to others by crossing over the center line. Even here though, I prefer the right most lane. It is the furthest from oncoming traffic.

On highways or out of town – Lane selection in these situations is addressed in the chapter entitled Controlled-Access Highways.

LIMITED VISIBILITY DUE TO TIME OF DAY AND WEATHER

It is a good idea to always have your headlights on at dawn and dusk, even if you can see well enough to drive safely. This makes your vehicle more visible to other drivers that may not see as well as you. Turning on the headlights will also turn on the tail lights. This makes you more visible to those behind you. Most all cars nowadays have daytime running lights. While daytime running lights are on all the time, the tail lights generally only come on with the headlights. There generally are no daytime running lights to the rear. Also, use the headlights when it is raining or any other time that visibility is limited such as by dust or fog. Unless the fog is very light you shouldn't be driving at all. If you suddenly encounter fog, and it is thick, put on your four-way flashers in addition to the headlights, and pull off the roadway as soon as you can do so safely.

NIGHT DRIVING

You know how moths are attracted to bright lights? They will even fly into a candle flame. Do you enjoy looking at a fire at the beach or at a campfire? We humans can even be mesmerized by a forest fire. Must be something we have in common with moths. However, when driving at night and you see headlights approaching, avoid looking directly at them even though you may be tempted to do so. Looking directly at the headlights will temporarily blind you. Not a good thing. You may want to look to decide whether they are on high beams or low. Don't do it. Keep your eyes directed at the right side of your roadway. Your peripheral vision will let you know where the oncoming vehicle is.

Some folks will suggest to quickly flash your high beams to alert the other driver. This might work but even that may not be a good idea as it may temporarily blind him. There are several reasons that the other headlights may appear to be on high even though they are not. Improperly adjusted lights, or an over-loaded car trunk or bed of a pickup can cause this. Or the other vehicle may be coming up a small rise. It will happen. Best to just look off to the right a bit.

GIVING AND GETTING THE RIGHT OF WAY

Suppose you are at an unlighted four-way intersection. As you approach, there are vehicles approaching from all the other three roadways. You all stop pretty much at the same time. Who goes first? General rules: the first vehicle to stop goes first; the vehicle on your right goes before you; the vehicle signaling a turn across the intersection goes after the straight-through traffic. But, you must be given the right of way, you cannot take it. Use eye contact. If you believe another vehicle should go first, and you have eye contact, motion them to go first. If another driver signals you to go, start to move forward. You can wave "thank you" as you pass through the intersection but do not do so before starting across. Otherwise your thank you wave may be misinterpreted as a "no – you go ahead" wave.

TRAFFIC CIRCLES

Sometimes called round-abouts. These are becoming more common. Some have one lane and some have two. I have never seen a good reason to be in the inside lane. You are only going to be in the lane for a few seconds. Changing into the inside lane and then back again to the outside lane to exit seems unnecessarily hazardous.

Most drivers do well with traffic circles. Traffic engineers' studies indicate that traffic moves better and there are fewer accidents compared with intersections. To make the turn you must enter a traffic circle at a lower speed than you might at an intersection. This lower speed makes the circle less dangerous. However, just as intersections have red light runners, traffic circles also have their hazardous drivers. Sometimes a driver coming into a circle will enter without looking at the traffic already in or partly into another entrance. Be sure to look for traffic already in the circle and for any possible vehicles that might not yield entering from your right. A vehicle approaching the circle at a high rate of speed will probably not yield. When in doubt, wait for another turn and then don't hesitate. If there is more than one lane, stay in the outside one.

SLOW MOVING VEHICLES

Sometimes you will be stuck behind a slow-moving vehicle. It could be that the driver is elderly or inexperienced, the vehicle isn't capable of going any faster, or any of a number of reasons. When it is safe to do so, simply pass it. Sometimes you may be behind it for quite a while because traffic on your left doesn't allow you to move over. Remember to always remain calm. Don't let another driver cause you to take unnecessary risks in trying to get around that vehicle. However, if you suspect that the slow driver is drunk or otherwise poses a danger and isn't just an overly cautious driver, stay behind. Either get off the roadway and wait awhile, or take other steps to avoid being in front of that driver. If he is posing a danger because of his driving, call it in to the local authorities. Be sure to give a description of the vehicle, the roadway and direction of travel and, if possible, the license plate # and state. And do it safely, not while driving. Or have a passenger call it in.

MISSING A TURN

Sometimes you will be in the wrong lane to safely make an exit or turn where you intended. Do not do what you will see many others do. I have seen many drivers swerve from two and three lanes over, at the last possible second, to make an exit in a high-speed traffic situation, cutting in front of me or others. Saving a few minutes or even a half an hour isn't worth risking your life. Taking the next exit, even one miles away, is still quicker than filling out an accident report, taking a trip to the hospital, or worse. Relax. Your college will still be there when you arrive, your friends and family will understand if you are late. Remember, what is the safer choice? Risk your life or take the next exit? Always take the safer alternative.

PARKING LOTS

Large, busy parking lots, such as found at Costco and Walmart, can pose hazards to pedestrians, and a challenge to your driving. I don't know what it is about parking lots but folks will walk in front of moving vehicles, almost as if they weren't there. Worse, they will walk behind you, even with small children, when you are backing out of a parking space.

Children may also run in front of you, or behind you, when trying to catch up with another child or parent. When possible, pull into a parking space where you can drive straight out rather than backing out. It is safer. Sometimes it is practical to back into a parking space so that you can drive straight out rather than backing out. People tend not to walk into a parking space to get around you while you are backing up. But they will walk behind you when you are backing out into a driving lane. When backing out, watch for another vehicle backing out from a space behind you as well. Look at the vehicles next to you and across from you to see if there are any drivers inside. Usually that means they will either get out of the vehicle, or drive out.

BACKING OUT OF PRIVATE DRIVEWAYS

Many homes have short driveways that require backing out of the garage or driveway. Every so often I have read or heard of a person backing over their own or their neighbor's child. I cannot imagine a more traumatic, heart-breaking accident. Always walk around the back of your vehicle before backing out to see if there are any children anywhere near you. Are there any children on tricycles or running about? It only takes an extra few seconds to make sure there are no children that might get behind you. While rear view cameras are a great help, they only show what is currently directly behind you, not who might be approaching from either side.

Chapter 6

INTERSECTIONS

GENERAL NOTES

INTERSECTIONS ARE DANGEROUS PLACES. Some of the worst accidents occur in intersections. Traffic approaches from four, sometimes five, directions. You must not only look for vehicle traffic but also for pedestrians and bicyclists. Occasionally there will be a train crossing as well. While most vehicles offer good protection from a frontal or rear collision, there is little protection from a side impact. There is a very small crumple zone to absorb the impact from a crash into the driver's or passenger's door. Entering and leaving an intersection requires your full-time attention.

The Manual of Uniform Traffic Control Devices is used throughout the U.S. for consistency in traffic control devices. Every so often it is updated. This consistency makes it a lot easier for us to drive around the country and feel comfortable that we understand most of the traffic control devices. However, each municipality, township, county and state highway district will still have their own conventions especially concerning intersections. Turn lanes, signal

97

patterns, crosswalk depictions, leading vs. lagging turn indicators and other devices for traffic control will vary from one community to another.

Some studies have shown that 25% of drivers don't use their turn signals when making turns while 50% don't signal when changing lanes. Where I live, most everyone signals most of the time. But apparently, this is not the case in all localities. Be alert for the possibility that the vehicle approaching from another direction may turn in front of you even though there is no turn signal. Always use your turn signals to alert other drivers of your intentions.

A green light means that you may go, not that you should go! You should only go when you are sure there is no vehicle about to speed through the intersection despite who has the right of way.

APPROACHING AN INTERSECTION

Seems like a simple proposition. Light is green, go through; light is red, stop; yellow, probably stop. Well, it is not that simple. Not if you want to be as safe as possible, avoid accidents and not run over anyone. Let's go through a few scenarios.

You are approaching a four-way intersection, the light is red. There are three lanes in each direction. You are in the center lane. There is a tractor-trailer stopped in the left lane. You are slowing down and are about 10 car lengths from the stop line when the light turns green. What do you do? Do you proceed through? The answer depends on a few more factors. Suppose there is a person still crossing in front of the tractor-trailer. Perhaps there is someone in a wheel chair or an adult with a couple of children in the crosswalk. Can you see if there is? No, because you cannot see the entire crosswalk in front of the truck. If you knew they were there, you would stop. If you wouldn't stop, stop reading this book and go directly to jail. Seriously, if the truck doesn't move when the light changes, there are a few reasons this might occur.

Is the truck looking to make a left turn? Does he have a turn signal on? If no turn signal, is he just slow getting started? Tractor-trailers are slow at the start line, sometimes going through three gears just to clear the intersection. But suppose there is someone crossing in front of the truck. You have got to stop or at least continue to slow down until you know there is no one there and that it is safe to continue. Either the truck will begin to move forward into the pedestrian walkway or it will remain stopped. If stopped, you need to know why before you cross the walkway.

Same scenario as above. You are approaching the intersection and the light turns green. This time the truck moves forward into the intersection. You now know that the cross walk is clear. Is it ok to continue through as cross traffic will be stopped? Well, maybe. Anytime you are entering an intersection, whether from a stop or approaching on a green light, you need to make a quick glance both left and right. You are looking for potential red-light runners. Some folks will run a red light trying to beat the light. Others will run the light simply because they are not paying attention.

You will see many red-light runners in your driving years. Maybe not for a long time or perhaps you will see two in one day, as I recently have. But, sooner or later, someone will run the light, putting you and maybe your loved ones at risk of injury or death. The only way to prevent this is to always look for them. Just do it. It will become second nature. Something your subconscious will remind you to do, or even do for you. If the tractor-trailer is blocking your view of any potential red-light runner from the left, use the tractor-trailer as a blocker. Do not pass it until you clear the intersection.

INTERSECTIONS WITH TRAFFIC LIGHTS

Some intersections have a traffic light for each lane and include one for the left turn lane. Others may have only one light for all lanes.

Different Light Durations – Remember that we talked about your subconscious taking over the more mundane aspects of driving, such as staying in the center of your lane? Well, your subconscious will also keep track of how long the yellow light will stay on before changing to red. It will do so based on the traffic lights where you drive most frequently.

Suppose you are approaching an intersection and the light turns yellow. Your subconscious tells you that you have enough time to clear the intersection before the light changes to red. This subconscious determination is based upon the yellow light duration where you normally drive. However, suppose you are entering an intersection that has a shorter yellow light duration. This can cause a real problem and could result in your running a red light.

Where I live in Coeur d'Alene, Idaho the yellow light duration is somewhat shorter than where I previously lived in Mesa, Arizona. This difference was noticeable and is probably the result of different speed zones requiring different light durations. To avoid risking an accident, stop any time the

101

light turns yellow while you are within stopping distance. Don't try to just "squeak by" the light. If you were driving within the posted speed limit, you will be able to stop safely.

Another variation which occurs is the light timing between opposing traffic lanes. Usually when one lane's light changes to red, the traffic waiting to cross will have a delay of a few seconds before the green signal. But, in some intersections the change will be simultaneous. Whenever you get the green signal to go, look to make sure there is no other vehicle about to enter from a cross street.

Leading/Lagging Left Turn Signals – Some localities will have a left turn signal that allows the turning lane to proceed before the through traffic lanes (leading left). This allows traffic from both your lane and the opposing turning lane to safely make a left turn without worrying about oncoming traffic. Other localities will have lagging left turns. The left turn signal will come on after all through traffic on your right has proceeded through the intersection. The traffic approaching from across the intersection will, most commonly, also have the same signal timing allowing them to first travel straight through and then, when through traffic has a red light, allow left turn traffic to proceed.

If you are used to seeing a green turn signal first, your subconscious will prompt you to make your left as soon as the light is green. This can happen if the light isn't a green left turn but just a round green signal for straight through traffic. Through traffic approaching in the opposing lanes will have the right of way. You must yield to all traffic before making your turn. As you can see, you need to pay conscious attention to traffic lights and not allow your subconscious to "take over" when in intersections. You don't want to make a left turn into oncoming traffic. Your subconscious is a great help in many areas of driving but intersections need your full-time conscious attention.

No Left Turn Signals – Some intersections will not have any left turn signals. This means that you can make a left turn on a green light, but only when there is no opposing traffic approaching from the other direction and there is no red arrow pointing left. This situation is the cause of many bad accidents. Often, someone turns left into opposing traffic and an approaching vehicle impacts the passenger door area. Even a 25 mile-an-hour impact into the side of most vehicles can result in serious or fatal injuries. Once again, the subconscious can be part of the cause. If you are used to leading left-turn signals in your home town and you now want to turn left in an intersection that has no left-turn signal, you need to be super alert. When the light turns green for your traffic, your subconscious may be saying it is ok to turn. It may not be. Don't drive on auto pilot when in intersections. Always be super alert.

Traffic Dependent Traffic Signals – Just to make intersection driving more interesting, traffic signals that have left turn signals will sometimes not give you a green turn light. Some lights are programmed to give a left turn signal only when there are three or more vehicles in the left turn lane. I suppose the reasoning is that one or two vehicles can make it safely through, after the opposing lanes get a red light, but three cannot. This usually results in the two vehicles entering the intersection and waiting for the yellow or red light before making the turn. If you wait for a second light change more traffic will probably build up behind you and you will get a turn signal the next time around. Otherwise you must enter the intersection on the green signal and wait till the end of the green signal, making a left turn on the yellow. Remember to not turn your wheels to the left until you are actually moving into the turn. Keep the wheels straight ahead. This way, if you are struck from behind while stopped, you won't be pushed into opposing traffic.

Many newer intersections have what are referred to as "smart" lights. These lights will adjust the turn and through-traffic light timing dependent on the number of approaching vehicles in each lane. Following the posted speed limits will generally allow you to reach following intersections while the lights are green. Traffic engineers pattern these light sequences to provide for the most efficient flow of traffic. Speeding will just cause you to get more red lights. One problem that can arise with these "smart" lights is that the traffic sensor might not give a left turn signal when a motorcycle is the first vehicle in line. It won't "see" the motorcycle as traffic. If this occurs, and you are behind the motorcycle, just wait it out. Sooner or later the motorcycle will turn left when traffic allows.

Inoperative or Flashing Traffic Lights – Sometimes you will encounter an intersection where there are traffic signals but they are not working. This usually occurs because of a lightning strike during a storm or an accident where someone hit a power supply for the signals. All traffic should stop and follow the common practice of giving the right of way to the first to arrive. Remember, you must be given the right of way, you can't just take it. Sometimes the lights will be flashing red for one roadway and yellow for the intersecting one.

On the main north/south highway in my hometown, the lights are set to flashing after 10pm. The main north/south traffic lanes get the yellow lights while the smaller, intersecting roadways get the flashing red. The lighter traffic during the nighttime hours flows better with this light pattern than it would if the lights were timed. Sometimes when the intersection lights aren't working properly, local police or traffic personnel will set the lights to flashing until the timing can be repaired.

INTERSECTIONS WITHOUT TRAFFIC LIGHTS

There are numerous intersections without traffic lights. Some will have traffic signs for all intersecting roads. One example is a four way stop. All traffic approaching must first stop before continuing through. Common driving practice is to allow the first vehicle to stop to be the first to proceed through the intersection. Some states provide that the first to stop has the right of way. Not all drivers will follow this rule. Remember, you cannot take the right of way – it has to be given. Most drivers are courteous in these situations but you shouldn't insist on the right of way. Be cautious and courteous to allow another to move through the intersection. Avoid confusing hand signals. If you are going to wave "Thank you" when you are given a hand signal to go, wait until you are almost through the intersection. Your early "thank you" may be interpreted as a "go ahead" signal to the other driver. Try to make eye contact with the other driver when determining when you or the other person should proceed.

Some intersections will have stop signs for one intersecting roadway with no signs for the other roadway. This is common where a main roadway has the right of way while the side street traffic is required to stop and yield to all traffic on the main roadway.

Some intersections, like some in my home town, have no traffic lights or traffic signs. These are found in residential sections where the speed limits are low. All traffic can proceed without stopping. This seems a bit scary, but I haven't experienced any problems. Probably the low traffic numbers and mutual driver nervousness make these intersections relatively safe. Common courtesy and common sense give the first driver approaching the intersection the right of way.

And just to make unlighted intersections a bit more interesting, some will have a stop or yield sign that you cannot see because of trees or other foliage. When you approach an intersection that has trees or other foliage blocking your view to a possible stop or yield sign, what should you do? Anytime you are approaching an intersection, you need to determine who has the right of way. If you cannot see if there is a stop or yield sign facing you, slow down and look across the intersection to the left side of the roadway. You are looking for the back of a yield or stop sign which would be facing the traffic approaching from the opposite direction. It won't be blocked from your view by foliage. If there is one, it is a pretty good bet that you have the same one facing you. The stop sign is an octagon while the yield sign is an upside-down triangle, remember? As you have slowed enough to either stop or yield, you will see the sign facing you in time to do either. What you don't want to do is drive blindly into the intersection. Don't assume that you have the right of way, simply because you don't see any stop or yield signs. You should see one of these, either facing you or the cross traffic. While there are some intersections that will have neither, they are rare. If there are none, you will need to slow down in time to avoid any traffic entering from either side.

STOPPING

When stopping in the left lane where there is no broad median separating opposing traffic, stop at least one-half vehicle length behind the crosswalk or stop line. Drivers approaching from your right, and making a left turn in front of you, will often cut partially into your lane. Cutting the turn too tight is a bit reckless, and unfortunately, very common. To avoid the chance of being struck on the left front of your vehicle, stay a bit back from the line giving the left turn driver a little extra room.

Sometimes you will see that a tractor-trailer is waiting at the light on the roadway to your right. If it is in the left turn lane, stop even further back, perhaps a whole car length, to allow it to make the turn. Even though the tractor will make a wide turn, clearing your vehicle by a wide margin, the trailer will make a tighter turn than the tractor. Staying further back is both common sense and a courtesy that will be appreciated. Most trailers of any type will make a sharper turn than the towing vehicle.

When stopping behind another vehicle, stop so that you can see where the tires of that vehicle touch the road. This gives enough room so that if you are hit from behind, you may have enough space to avoid hitting the vehicle in front, reducing the total impact to your vehicle and to you. Sometimes the vehicle in front will stall or become disabled. Staying further back will give you enough room to get around that vehicle rather than being stuck behind it. Leave this extra room whenever stopping behind another vehicle, not just at intersections.

STOPPING AT TRAIN CROSSINGS

Sometimes train crossings will be found at intersections along with intersecting roadways. There are many variations of traffic control signs and barriers for railroad crossings.

Some crossings will have multiple lights, barriers and signs. Others, especially in rural areas, will have only one sign, no lights and no barriers. A couple of problems can occur when train crossings are part of intersections. Always stop a few car lengths before the tracks if there is traffic in front of you. Assuming you have the right to cross the tracks, wait until there is plenty of room behind the traffic in front before crossing. You don't want to be stopped on the tracks while waiting for the traffic in front to move. Also, do not ever drive around barriers that are blocking the tracks. Even though one train has passed and the barrier hasn't lifted, do not assume it isn't working. There may be another train coming.

This exact scenario occurred in an accident investigated by another trooper in my area. Apparently, the business commuter thought it was safe to go around the barriers as one train had passed. He began to cross but was broadsided by a second train.

Suppose for a moment that the barrier isn't working and there is no other train? Stay behind the barrier. You can always turn around. You may be late for any number of appointments that won't matter in a few years. But you will be alive. Being hit by a train will take more time out of your day what with filling out all the paperwork for a police report and an insurance claim. That is if you are still around to do so.

POTENTIAL HAZARDS

There are many hazards in and around intersections. Here are a few. I'm sure as you gain experience you will add more to watch for.

Red-Light Runners – We talked about looking for red light runners when we discussed approaching an intersection. What about when first driving forward after being stopped? Suppose you are stopped in the left lane of two lanes in your direction. Now suppose you cannot see the traffic lanes approaching from the right due to a large truck on your right. The light changes to green. The truck is a tractor-trailer and you know it will be slow getting started. You are driving a sporty car that will run circles around the truck. Do you just tromp on the gas and show what a fast car you have?

No, you don't. You use the truck as a "blocker". A blocker is a vehicle that stays between you and any potential red-light runner. It will prevent a red-light runner, that you cannot see, from smashing into your vehicle. If it is going to hit anyone it will be the truck, not you. He can see a potential red-light runner from the right, you cannot. Stay alongside the truck until you are across the intersection. Do the same

111

when in a lane with a larger vehicle to your left blocking your view to traffic approaching from that side. See the following diagram.

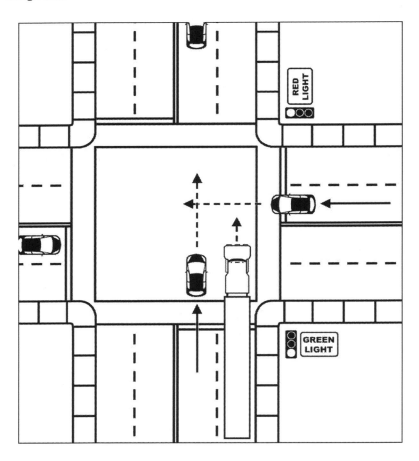

This one tip kept my son Chris from being broadsided shortly after he received his driver's license.

Pedestrians – Pedestrians come in every age, size and ability to walk, jump, run or otherwise cross intersections.

112

Children especially require special attention. Watch for them, not only when they are in the crosswalks, but also anytime they are near your vehicle. Sometimes they will spontaneously run into a traffic lane or crosswalk, whether running to greet someone, to recover a ball or pet, or just because they are children. Always give them the benefit of extra caution. Elderly folks and folks in wheel chairs require extra time to cross. Give them extra attention as well.

Bicyclists – In this next drawing, you are in the right lane, approaching an intersection with a green light. You just passed a bicyclist on your right, who is either in a bike lane, on the right side of your lane or even on the sidewalk. You wish to turn right so you are slowing down, while the bicyclist is continuing at a constant speed.

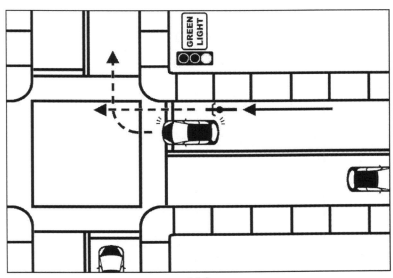

It appears that he might continue through the intersection or that he might turn right. You don't know what he intends to do. Make sure he either stops to let you turn, or wait for him to pass you before turning. Don't assume he has seen your turn signal and will yield. On occasion I have seen a bicyclist on the sidewalk, riding in my direction, drive from the sidewalk onto the roadway at the intersection, cross in the traffic lane, and then return to the sidewalk once across. Anytime you see a bicyclist, pay extra attention.

Motorcyclists – These folks need all the help they can get to stay safe in traffic. The chance of dying while riding a motorcycle is about 40 times greater than that of an occupant in a motor vehicle. No, that is not a typo. This is especially true of passengers on motorcycles. They are basically sitting in what I see as an ejection seat. They have even less of a chance of surviving a motorcycle accident than the driver. Parents, are you paying attention? Please forbid your beautiful sons and daughters from riding on motorcycles until they are 40 or so. If your child convinces you, through tears and promises of safety, that they need to ride, get them helmets, boots, gloves, wrist and knee pads and as much safety gear as you can find. Then buy them an under-powered, nerdy looking motor bike that will embarrass them with their friends and put an end to the idea of ever riding a motorcycle, at least in traffic. If you weaken and let them ride, make it off-road only.

I have investigated many motorcycle/vehicle accidents but remember just a few where the fault lay solely with the motorcyclist. Most times the motorcyclist did nothing wrong. Still, who do you suppose got the worst of it? A large percentage of the accidents occurred when a vehicle pulled out from a cross street or a driveway directly into the motorcyclist's path. Many times, the vehicle driver said he or she never saw the motorcycle. This often happened in broad daylight, on sunny days with an unobstructed view, as well as in the rain and at night. I have since learned why this might occur.

Some drivers do not consciously look for motorcycles, just trucks and cars. This isn't a desire to not see motorcyclists, bicyclists, or even pedestrians. It's not intentional. Once again, our subconscious is sorting through a myriad of information and only giving our conscious mind the "important" details for the task at hand. This phenomenon is known as "Inattentional Blindness". We will talk about this in the chapter on Defensive Driving. If your subconscious mind only sees other cars and trucks as hazards to you, it will only forward those to the conscious mind. The conscious mind will only "see" cars and trucks. This is especially true if you are momentarily distracted for whatever reason. You must think "Any cars or trucks; bicyclists; pedestrians; motorcyclists; animals; debris such as tire treads in my path?" Only when you train your subconscious to look for all potential hazards will your subconscious forward these hazards to your conscious mind. Think about these potential hazards consciously and your subconscious will get the message. Then you will truly "see" all potential hazards. The subconscious is kind of scary, isn't it? It is a great help when driving. You just need to teach it what is important.

When following motorcyclists, give them more room that you do for cars and trucks. Lots of road conditions that have little or no noticeable effect on a car or truck can seriously affect the traction of a motorcycle. Water, gravel, slick oily spots and even painted lane markings reduce a motorcycle's ability to maintain traction. Potholes and uneven lanes, as well as roadway seams, all play havoc with keeping a motorcycle ride smooth and safe. Remember all the factors we addressed about maintaining traction of tires to the road? Maintaining traction is a whole lot more difficult on a motorcycle.

I occasionally rode a motorcycle on roadways when I was 22 or so. I still ride off road occasionally but no more on roadways. Had I been a motorcyclist when I became a state trooper, I would have given it up eventually. However,

because of one day in my 20's, I gave it up early on. Here's
why.

> *While driving about 50 miles an hour on a parkway,*
> *a driver cut in front of me, missing my front tire by*
> *no more than a foot or so. He probably didn't think*
> *he was being careless but it shook me up a bit. Laying*
> *my bike down while doing 50 probably would have*
> *put a damper on my morning. However, the next*
> *incident that same day caused me to give up riding*
> *on public roadways forever.*
>
> *I was stopped at a light in the left of two lanes in my*
> *direction. It was early on a Monday morning and the*
> *weather was clear. There was a truck stopped to my*
> *right. Across the intersection there were two lanes of*
> *traffic also stopped at the light. At the inside, or left*
> *lane, there was a pickup. When the light changed, the*
> *pickup came across the center lane straight towards*
> *me. I looked at the driver. He was looking directly at*
> *me. He was smiling! SMILING! There is no doubt he*
> *saw me and, for whatever reason, looked like he*
> *planned to run over me. I quickly glanced to my right.*
> *The truck driver to my right saw what was happening*
> *and drove to his right, onto the shoulder, giving me*
> *room to move over. The pickup sped off, returning to*

> *his proper lane. Why did this happen? I have no Idea.*
> *I had recently been discharged from the Navy and*
> *hadn't yet had time to make any serious enemies. I*
> *didn't become a state trooper for another five years so*
> *he wasn't a disgruntled arrestee. He was a total*
> *stranger. Maybe he mistook me for a mortal enemy or*
> *maybe he was a homicidal maniac. Maybe he was*
> *just having a bad hair day. In any event, these two*
> *incidents caused me to give up riding a motorcycle in*
> *traffic.*

It only takes one accident to put you six feet under. I have always tried really hard to put that off for as long as possible. Giving up riding on public roadways seemed like a good way to improve my odds. Parents – you still with me? No motorcycles!

Chapter 7

CONTROLLED-ACCESS HIGHWAYS

THERE ARE SOME SITUATIONS that you will encounter on controlled-access highways that do not occur in cities and towns. Controlled-access highways are roadways which have specific on-ramps and off-ramps such as freeways and parkways. There are no cross streets. Sometimes you must pay tolls, the amount dependent upon how far you drive. Traffic moves faster than in town so it helps to know what to expect before it occurs. The various designs of on-ramps and off-ramps require attention as some create more risks than others. Choice of lane usage will vary with the number of lanes in each direction. Lane usage choice will also vary when in rural areas compared with passing through cities.

ON- AND OFF-RAMPS

Different design on- and off-ramps – There are numerous on- and off-ramp designs but most fall into two categories - the **diamond** and the **cloverleaf.**

- **Diamond** – A diamond-shaped designed interchange will have an off-ramp before the overpass for the intersecting

119

roadway. The on-ramp from that same cross roadway will be after the overpass. This allows traffic wishing to exit to do so before the on-ramp traffic enters the highway. This design allows traffic to exit and to enter without crossing in front of other traffic. See the following diagram.

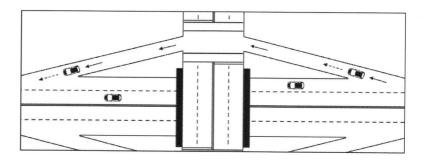

- **Cloverleaf** – The cloverleaf design requires the traffic wishing to exit the highway to pass under the cross highway before exiting. Unfortunately, the traffic wishing to enter the highway must do so before the overpass roadway. This means that the traffic wishing to exit and the traffic wishing to enter must cross each other's path while entering and exiting. This can make for some exciting and hazardous driving. See the following diagram.

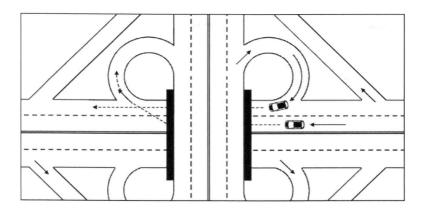

You need to use extra caution when entering or exiting in a clover-leaf ramp design. The older roadways tend to have the cloverleaf design, especially those found in urban areas. The newer, diamond design is found on newer highways and in more rural areas, where there is room for the larger interchange.

Long vs. short on- and off-ramps – Some ramps allow ample time to get up to speed allowing you to merge safely into traffic. The diamond shape ramps will tend to have longer and straighter on- and off-ramps, allowing for easier entry to and exit from controlled-access highways. The cloverleaf ramps, due to design, will be shorter and curved, making it more difficult to enter and exit as safely. This also causes a more limited view to traffic already on the highway. Recognize what the design is when entering and exiting and act accordingly. You will have less time to safely enter and exit cloverleaf interchanges than you will with diamond designs. Recognizing the different designs will eliminate surprises and better prepare you for a safer entry and exit.

ENTERING THE HIGHWAY

Allow as much room as possible between yourself and the vehicle in front when on the on-ramp for a controlled access highway. You want enough room so that you can accelerate as rapidly as is necessary to merge. If you leave too little room, the vehicle in front may accelerate too slowly for you to safely enter on-coming traffic. On rare occasions, the vehicle in front may even stop at the end of the on-ramp. You want to be far enough behind to allow for this.

Sometimes the vehicle behind you will be driven by an impatient or simply reckless driver. He will crowd you on the ramp, and then as soon as there is enough room, will immediately pull next to you on your left, sometimes even when still on the on-ramp. He will eliminate your ability to move to the second lane on your left, even though you have your left turn signal on. Expect it and it won't surprise you. He is a hazard to be avoided. Let him go and move over when you can.

SELECTION OF LANES

What lane should you be in? Depends on how many lanes there are and whether you are in a congested area or in a rural area. It also depends upon your experience and comfort level with high speed driving. Imagine a six-lane highway, three lanes in each direction, separated by a barrier or median. If you are planning to exit shortly you should be in the right lane. When not planning to exit, I suggest that you drive in the center lane. The speeders will mostly be on your left and the merging and entering traffic will be on your right. You can always move left or right if necessary, and you won't be crowded by speeders and tailgaters.

If there are more lanes, say six in each direction, stay in lanes two, three or four. As you gain experience you may feel more comfortable in the left, or number one, lane. The advantage of the left lane is that there will be no vehicles crossing in front. There will be no danger from any vehicle on the left as there will be none. The disadvantage is that the speed is greater and there will always be someone that will want to go faster, no matter the speed limit. When safe to do so, signal that you will move over to let him go by. Do not speed up to make more room between the two of you as he will most likely just speed up as well.

I will drive in the left lane of multiple lanes when traffic is relatively light. This makes it easy to move right to let faster traffic pass me and then return to the faster lane. Until you get a lot of experience driving and are comfortable with your vehicle's handling characteristics, the center, slower lanes are a safer bet.

Sometimes, where two controlled-access highways merge, there may be six or more lanes in your direction. This is where knowing how far it is to your next exit becomes doubly important. You also need to know on which side of the roadway your exit is located. Most exits, by far, are on the right. But, just to make driving more interesting, an exit will occasionally be on the left. If you are on the wrong side of the multiple lanes when your exit arrives, make the safe decision to go past it and take the next exit. High speed traffic is no place to make sudden, multiple-lane changes.

If you are on a highway with just two lanes in each direction, lane choice will depend on traffic. Generally, as an inexperienced driver, you should drive in the right lane in rural areas. You can move left, if there are tractor-trailers or other slower moving traffic in the right lane, returning to the right lane after passing. However, when approaching congested areas around cities, the left lane is the safer bet. Usually the speed limits will be lower within city limits. The right lane will have traffic entering and exiting so the left lane will be easier, safer driving. Sometimes the roadway in and around cities will have additional lanes so that you can drive in the center lane, returning to the right lane when back in rural areas.

HOV LANES

HOV is an abbreviation for High Occupancy Vehicle. HOV lanes are also known as Carpool Lanes. These lanes are on the left of all other lanes and are reserved for multiple occupancy vehicles. Sometimes there are certain hours when all traffic may use these lanes. At other times this lane will be reserved for multiple occupancy vehicles only. The regulations for these lanes will vary from state to state and sometimes within a state. The restrictions regarding these lanes should be posted along the left side of the roadway. On certain highways, in California for example, you may not enter or exit an HOV lane except in specially marked areas. Other states will allow entering and exiting at any time. You are responsible for knowing what the laws are, in whatever state you are. Moving into and out of HOV lanes incorrectly can result in a significant fine.

I will use the HOV lane if the traffic is very light. It is a safer lane as there will be no traffic to the left. I will also use it if the traffic is very heavy, moving slowly. This slower traffic will be found mostly during the rush hours on week days. If you do use the HOV lane there is one danger to watch for, especially in those states that allow entry at any time. Occasionally a vehicle will move into the much faster HOV lane from the lane to the right, possibly creating a hazard. Be especially aware of this possibility. Be prepared to brake. You should never drive more that 10 or 15 miles faster than an adjoining lane, whether on a controlled-access highway or elsewhere. It is too risky. Sometimes, the traffic in the other lanes will be stopped or practically stopped. Legally, you may drive the speed limit, maybe 60 mph or so. But doing so is dangerous if any other vehicle comes into your lane from the stopped lanes.

Some folks who are not permitted to be in the HOV lane will enter it anyway. Also, don't let some hotrod behind you push you to go faster. Move over and let him by when you can do so safely. Let him know you will move over by signaling.

Another advantage of the HOV lane is the occasional opportunity to exit on the left. This will eliminate the need to cross multiple lanes to the right to do so. It helps if you know where these left exits are before you reach them.

DEBRIS IN ROADWAYS

You will see all kinds of debris on the highway. Not necessarily often but still often enough to create a problem if it is in your path. The most common debris is pieces of tire tread, sometimes called "road alligators". These are from large truck tires that have been retreaded after the original tread has worn. Sometimes pieces of this retread material will come off and lie in the roadway. Eventually it will work its way to the side of the roadway due to traffic driving over it. You don't want to be the one to drive over it. The pieces tend to be large. As you can imagine, they are of a pretty hard material. They can cause damage to the undercarriage of your vehicle and might even become stuck there. Avoid them, but don't blindly move into another lane to avoid them. If you find yourself in a situation that you will run over a piece of tire tread, try to center your vehicle over it to avoid contact with your tires. It might damage something under the vehicle but you won't lose control of your vehicle which you might if it gets caught between a wheel and the frame of the car. If you maintain your safe distance behind traffic, you should be able to avoid all debris that might appear in your lane.

USE YOUR PASSENGER AS A NAVIGATOR

Until you are familiar with a particular highway and its exits, ask your passenger to help you with navigation. This person can keep you advised of which side of the roadway your exit will be as well as the distance to it. This will allow you to focus on traffic around you. This is especially important on highways with many lanes. Five lanes or so in each direction can be a real challenge. There will be many vehicles in your vicinity - some gaining on you - some changing into and out of your lane. Wondering on which side of the roadway your exit is, and how far it is, are distractions you don't need. If you don't have a navigator, and you are not familiar with the road, look up the exit you need before starting your drive. Know the name or number of the exit before the one you want so that you will know when yours is next.

SIGNALING

Always signal your intentions. Traffic moving at 65 miles an hour will move at about 100 feet a second. Give all drivers around you plenty of notice that you intend to change lanes. Then, when moving over, make sure that no other vehicle is moving into that lane as well. Some drivers will not signal lane changes. Watch for any indication that another vehicle is about to change lanes as well. A vehicle, in a lane next to you, that is drifting towards your lane is an indication that it may move into your lane, with or without signaling.

DRIVING PATTERNS

When the traffic is light to moderate, you may notice "bunching". This is where there will be perhaps 10 or more vehicles that seem to be traveling together. Let's call that group of cars a "pack". Then there will be a long, empty stretch of highway with no traffic perhaps followed by another pack. These packs are caused by two or more slow moving vehicles in the lead followed by other drivers who wish to pass but are having a difficult time doing so. What is the safest place to be? Halfway between the packs. There is little reason to try to get through them. Just stay away from them and they will eventually disperse.

STOPPED VEHICLES

When you see a vehicle stopped on the shoulder of a highway, whether it is an emergency vehicle, police car or just an apparently disabled vehicle with people about, move out of the right lane as you pass. You will see tractor-trailer drivers do this consistently. It is a good safety measure.

EXITS

Sometimes you will be two or more lanes to the left of your exit and have just a short time to move into the exit lane. If there is no traffic anywhere near you it can be done safely. However, if you would have to cross in front of nearby traffic to make your exit and do not have enough time and distance to do so safely, go to the next exit. I have gone as much as twenty miles to the next exit because I was unfamiliar with the highway and couldn't make my exit safely. It was the safer choice. You should do likewise.

Some exits will have short off-ramps with yellow warning signs listing a suggested speed. These signs are designed by highway engineers and reflect what they believe is a safe exit speed for a dry roadway in good condition. If the roadway is wet or icy, your safe speed will be less. Some vehicles might be able to safely make the exit at somewhat higher speeds than the suggested speed. Other vehicles won't be able to do so safely. Heed the suggested speed. Over time you will notice many tire tracks and vehicle scrape marks on off-ramp guard rails and Jersey barriers on the outside of the turn. These were caused by drivers that couldn't safely make the exit or were distracted. Don't let one of these drivers push you into a higher exit speed than you would otherwise choose. Let the reckless drivers crash when they are by themselves.

Some exits will be downhill and have a short, tight turn to the right, as in a cloverleaf interchange. These require a much lower off-ramp speed than a long straight off-ramp. Remember all that information about maintaining control of your vehicle? Braking in a turn is trickier than braking in a straight line. Braking downhill also takes more distance. Braking too hard in a downhill turn can cause a drifting skid and risks a rollover. Plan accordingly when approaching an off-ramp. You should have slowed enough before entering the off-ramp so that additional braking during the exit will be minimal.

7 - Controlled Access Highways

Chapter 8

READING OTHER VEHICLES AND DRIVERS

SO FAR YOU HAVE LEARNED about the need to be familiar with your vehicle's handling capabilities and its overall maintenance. You have learned basic driving skills, to avoid distractions and to follow the written, as well as the unspoken, rules of the road. You have learned that road conditions and the weather can affect your ability to safely control your vehicle. These factors relate to you and how you should react to the situations. That is a lot to learn. It is not enough. The key to surviving on the road is defensive driving — looking out for the other driver, whose actions are out of your control.

Your goal is to get wherever you are going and not crash. If you were the only driver out there it would be a pretty safe place to be. But there are others, lots of others. There are good drivers, bad drivers, inexperienced and impaired drivers and perhaps the most common — temporarily inattentive drivers. At any given time, most drivers will not create a hazard. Some of them will pose a potential hazard and a few will become actual, immediate hazards. I always assume that 10% of the drivers I see will create a hazard to me. It keeps me alert. You should do likewise. My older son, who has been driving about 25 years now, thinks this estimate is too low.

Defensive driving techniques will be addressed in the next chapter. But recognizing that certain types of vehicles and drivers can pose a hazard to you is a good start to defensive driving in general. This chapter will show you how to spot potential problems posed by them. Once you recognize that a vehicle or driver can be a hazard, you will be able to minimize the danger to yourself. Recognizing the potential problems as they arise makes you safer. It is the unexpected hazard that poses the most serious risk. Always try to keep these to a minimum.

VEHICLES

The following listed vehicles can create hazardous situations just because of what they are, not because of drivers' actions.

Junkers – This is a vehicle that has a lot of dents or rust, or is just in poor shape. It may be putting out a lot of smelly exhaust. If it looks like it should be in a junkyard it belongs in this category. If it's poorly maintained on the outside, perhaps the suspension, steering or brakes are also in poor shape. Maybe it is in great mechanical condition but only looks like it is falling apart. What are the odds? I don't know either. Best to give it a little extra room.

Any Vehicle with Loose Loads – This is a vehicle that has perhaps a refrigerator upright in the back of a pickup which may be fastened in place with a few ropes or held in place by a person sitting on one rear fender. It could be a vehicle with a mattress, a sheet of plywood, pipes or other load tied or held onto the roof. Mattresses and sheets of plywood will not stay on the roof at highway speeds. Pipes can slide out from under ropes when the vehicle brakes or hits another. A pickup with any number of items in the bed that are not tied down fits this category. Stay way back of these, or in a different lane. I have seen bicycles, 55-gallon metal drums, a mattress, gas cans and many other items fall off or out of cars and trucks.

Gravel Trucks – Usually these are large dump trucks or even tractor-trailers. Even when covered, they tend to drop some of their load. The gravel may not even come from the actual load but be some that spilled onto the frame and undercarriage when loaded, which then comes loose when the truck first turns onto the roadway. While not a great hazard, gravel can easily crack your windshield. Makes a loud noise when it does, too.

Ice and Snow Covered Vehicles – When you see a vehicle that still has a lot of snow or ice on the roof, even though the rest of the vehicle is clean, stay clear. When those patches of snow and ice come off, and they will, you don't want to be behind it, or even on either side of it when it happens.

Rental Trucks – You should assume that the driver rented this truck for a short time and is not experienced with it. Give it some extra room.

Moving Billboards – These are vehicles that are large, such as a tractor-trailer or box truck. They are called "billboards" because they completely block your view to the front, including traffic lights. Following a tractor-trailer can sometimes be a good idea but don't follow so close that you are blinded to all traffic and traffic control devices. Either drop back or change lanes.

Highway Construction Vehicles – You will see these where the roadway is being repaired or widened. There will be barricades, signs and probably traffic-control people about. When you see these vehicles enter onto a roadway from a construction site give them some extra room. They will take a little longer to get up to speed and may even drop some loose rocks, gravel or dirt onto the roadway. Occasionally there may be a fist-sized rock stuck between dual tires in the rear. Usually these folks are good about checking their vehicles over before entering the roadway. Usually the truck will have "mud flaps" behind the rear tires which will deflect any pebbles, sand and small rocks. But if there is a rock stuck between the rear tires you don't want to be anywhere near it when it comes loose. It can be thrown backwards posing a hazard to any traffic behind. Give these vehicles extra leeway. The drivers will appreciate it and it will be safer for you.

Flat Bed Tow Trucks – Tow truck companies often use these for transporting disabled vehicles. Sometimes the bed of these tow trucks projects well behind the rear bumper to allow for the bed to be tilted down onto the roadway. They are not particularly hazardous but they are scary to be behind. If you are behind this vehicle at a light, or even in traffic, and are rear ended into that vehicle, you may be pushed into that sharp, steel bed well before either your bumper or that of the truck comes into play. Try not to be behind them, and if you do find yourself there, stay way back.

Any Vehicle with a Trailer – This category includes the towing of such things as boats, motorcycles, rental trailers for moving, toy haulers, landscaping debris, etc. Sometimes trailers will jack-knife, meaning the trailer will skid sideways into the next lane over. This can occur when the brakes on the towing vehicle are applied in a turn or when traveling downhill. The trailer will skid to one side or the other instead of tracking the towing vehicle. Often, when this sideways

137

skidding occurs, the trailer will end up crossways to the towing vehicle and then come loose or even overturn. Do not drive, for any extended time, behind a trailer or in the adjoining lane. If jack knifing occurs, you don't want to be alongside. Sometimes the taillights won't work. Sometimes, stuff will just fall off. Best to stay far back or in a non-adjoining lane.

Autonomous (Driverless) Vehicle – Driverless vehicles are being tested in several states. Until they have been thoroughly tested and accepted by the driving and safety experts, you should give them lots of room. They are being touted as being safe but whatever "brain" they might have will be no match for the reasoning power of the human brain, even your unfinished teen brain. When it comes to reasoning itself out of a situation not previously encountered or imagined by their programmers, I believe these autonomous vehicles will fail. They will be limited to the instructions which their programmers imagined. They can only react to those situations programmed into them. Even then, the programming will be at risk for electronic failures, unforeseen bugs and hacking, to mention just a few possible problems. I think it will be a long time before a robot will have the reasoning ability of a human. To be able to imagine, and then choose from, an unlimited selection of alternatives is still reserved for us humans. Maybe even some other animals. But not robots, yet. Give them some extra room.

This list is not all inclusive. You will add other vehicles to this list as you drive.

DRIVERS

All drivers are potential hazards to you although only a few will create an actual hazardous situation. Let's look at some drivers that need extra attention from you.

Impatient Driver – This guy is found mostly in town rather than on the highway. He will tend to tailgate you to get you to move over. He will race from light to light even if the traffic signal sequences require him to brake at every light. This is a driver to avoid. You don't want him behind you but don't speed just because he is crowding you. He will simply increase his speed and still tailgate you. Don't make any unannounced, sudden moves. Move over when it is safe to do so and use your signal to show him you are trying to get out of his way. If you are in heavy city traffic, you will usually catch up to him at some future traffic signal.

Tailgater – One study claimed that tailgaters cause 40% of accidents. I think these folks don't realize that tailgating is dangerous. They are in their own little world and don't see any danger in being a few feet off your rear bumper at highway speeds. I have noticed many teenagers, driving small, compact cars, doing this. These tailgaters don't generally drive aggressively or change lanes much. They seem to be content to just stay a few feet behind the car in front. Hopefully, with experience they will develop better driving skills.

There is a different type of tailgater that is aggressive. You will encounter him in town as well as on the highway. Don't speed up just to get rid of him. He will only speed up and continue to tailgate you.

If you are on a two-lane roadway when the tailgater appears, he probably wants to pass you. Where lane markings allow passing, slow down a bit and move to the right side of your lane. You can use a right turn signal, even though there is no right turn ahead. This should tell him that you see him and will make extra room for him to pass. Then, as he passes, slow a little more. This will give him room to return to your lane sooner. You will also encounter the tailgater in slower city traffic where is it not always feasible to move over. Perhaps there is only one lane, or you want to turn soon and you are in the correct lane to do so. In these cases, maintain a steady speed and don't make any sudden stops. Signal your intentions and stay calm.

Some folks will advise you to slow down, even to take your foot off the gas, hoping that the tailgater will go around you. Others will suggest lightly tapping your brake pedal to warn him off. Some drivers will turn on the windshield wipers. At highway speeds, some of the spray will reach the tailgater's windshield. Hopefully the tailgater will take that as a polite hint to back off. Any one of these tactics may work just fine most of the time. But if the tailgater is already in a "road rage", for whatever reason, any one of these tactics may make him even angrier. What is the safest way to eliminate this hazard? This is what you should ask yourself in any potentially hazardous situation. If I believe the tailgater can see me, I will reach up and act as if I am adjusting my rear-view mirror. Sometimes this will be enough for him to back off. If that doesn't work, I will signal that I will move over and let him pass.

Hotdog – You will encounter this driver on highways. There are a lot of driving moves that can be reckless but this driver takes reckless driving to a new level. Some drivers create an unintentional, brief hazard because of a lack of attention. This guy intentionally creates multiple hazardous situations, in rapid succession. The goal of the hotdog is to drive faster than overall traffic even if traffic is moving at the legal speed limit. He speeds. He constantly changes lanes. He will pull into and out of lanes within a few feet of other vehicles if there is an opening large enough for his vehicle. He will again switch lanes as soon as there is any chance that it will get him a few feet farther along. He usually won't signal. He tailgates. He is one of the most hazardous drivers out there. The only good thing about him is that he is easy to spot. Let this guy go around you or move over as you see him approaching. If you are going to change lanes as he is coming up behind you, give him plenty of notice by signaling so he doesn't move into that lane just before you do.

Magnetic Driver – A magnetic driver can be found on freeways and other highways. This is a driver who will come up from behind on the right or left and then stay in your blind spot, his front bumper about even with your rear tire. He will then match your speed, just sort of hanging there. I don't know what the psychological explanation is for this. Perhaps the driver is lazy and feels safe if he just matches your speed, relying on you to spot hazards. Maybe he just wants to relax and let you do the driving. I don't know why this occurs but you will encounter it. It is never a good idea for two vehicles to travel closely together for any distance. To eliminate this problem, change your speed slightly or move over. Put some distance between yourself and him.

Speeder – As you learned in the chapter on maintaining control of a vehicle, increased speed increases the forces affecting the driver's ability to control the vehicle. Someone driving faster than you will have a proportionately harder time controlling her vehicle. It is common on highways for most traffic to travel a few miles over the limit. On a freeway with a maximum speed of 65 you will find traffic moving at 67 or 68. In the left lane of an eight or ten lane freeway you will find most of the fastest drivers. If traffic is light enough some will travel 80 mph or more unless there are officers about. On a highway with three or more lanes in each direction you should be driving in the middle lanes. Most speeders will be to your left and shouldn't pose a danger to you. If one of these speeders gets right behind you, signal that you will move over and let him by but do so only when it is safe. While you will make allowances for other drivers, including speeders, don't drive in a less safe manner just to let them by.

Distracted/Inattentive Driver – This can be anyone. A recent study claims that texting, alone, is a leading cause of accidents – even more than drunk driving. Whether this is true is irrelevant. Just accept that driver distraction is a serious problem that has only gotten worse with cell phones. Talking hands-free on the phone has now been shown to be just as distracting as holding a phone to the ear. Anytime a driver is distracted, he can pose a hazard to you.

We talked about not being distracted when you are driving. You will see drivers doing everything I said you shouldn't. They will be looking at maps, reading the newspaper or even a book, putting on makeup, talking or texting on the phone, eating or taking any number of other actions that temporarily distracts them. I have seen many drivers making a turn with one hand while holding a phone to their ear with the other. These drivers pose a hazard to others near them. While most of them will pass by you without incident, it only takes one to hurt you.

Remember when we talked about braking distance at different speeds? The three parts of a stop include: 1) perception time, 2) reaction time, and 3) braking distance. Distracted drivers will have increased perception time and may have increased reaction time as well. Be aware of them and allow for it. Sometimes there isn't much you can do as they may be close to you for just a few seconds. If they are traveling in the same direction as you, distance yourself from them.

Intoxicated/Drugged Driver – It may take a lot of testimony in court to convict a person of driving while intoxicated as persons are "legally innocent" until proven guilty. This is true even though the driver is factually guilty. Most of us have seen people that we believe are drunk or under the influence of drugs. We will reach that conclusion within just a few seconds of seeing them or hearing them speak. We don't need a two- or three-day trial to reach that conclusion. When you see a driver who is driving erratically, assume he is guilty of something. It may be because of drugs, legal or otherwise. It may just be DWS, driving while stupid. He might be legally innocent but he would be creating an actual hazard. Act accordingly. You aren't accusing him of any crime, just doing your best to avoid becoming his victim. If you see a driver you suspect of being under the influence of alcohol or drugs because of his driving, you should accept that he is. He might be diabetic and suffering insulin shock or perhaps simply falling asleep. The cause doesn't matter. You are best off driving behind him rather than being in front. Much safer. Put lots of distance between yourself and him.

Elderly Folks – This section should be fun for the politically correct crowd. Not only am I profiling drivers by their actions and by what they drive, now I am adding the elderly. I make no excuses for including anyone on this list. My age at the time of writing this is 74. I exercise regularly, swim and don't have any major physical infirmities. But I don't believe I am as physically fit as I was in my youth. My eye tests show that I have 20/20 vision with slight corrective contacts. I recently had an eye test at the motor vehicle department when renewing my driver's license. The State of Idaho determined that I am still qualified to drive. I had mild cataracts at the time of my eye test. At night, they caused me to see small star bursts around lights. The lettering on street signs was a little fuzzy. So, having 20/20 vision doesn't mean that my vision is as good as that of a younger person who also has 20/20 vision. I have recently had one cataract removed and am scheduled to have the other removed as well. It remains to be seen if my nighttime vision returns to that of my youth. In any event, you can expect that us elderly folks don't see as well as you do.

My hearing also isn't as good as it was when I was younger. Have you ever seen a vehicle with its turn signal on for a long time, even though the vehicle doesn't turn? If you haven't, you will. Odds are that the driver is elderly. As we get older we sometimes lose the ability to hear the higher frequencies. This includes the sound of the turn signal. Sometimes we older folks just don't hear the turn signal so it remains on. My perception time for recognizing a hazard and my reaction time to that hazard may also have increased over that of my youth. I don't know whether this is true but it makes sense simply based upon my age.

Lots of elderly folks don't drive at night unless necessary. I suspect it is for the reasons I just mentioned. Give us a little extra room. We may need a little extra time to make turns or even to decide whether to turn.

Out-of-Stater – Anytime you see out-of-state plates, especially if the vehicle is from a non-adjoining state, expect that the driver may slow down at unexpected times. The driver might be lost or just looking for the correct exit or turn. Giving him a few extra feet of room is a good safety measure.

Slow Driver – There could be many reasons for this. Being super cautious, intoxicated, tired, or talking on the phone are just a few of the possible reasons. It could be a zombie driver. It doesn't matter why the person is driving slow. Sometimes when you are on a highway you may come up behind a much slower driver and get trapped there for a while because of faster traffic on either side. Accept that you may be there a while and then pass when the opportunity presents itself. Be careful when passing as the driver could be impaired and decide to change lanes just as you are passing.

Polite Talker – This is an interesting driver. This is a driver who is talking to a passenger in the right, front seat. He will turn to face the listener each time he speaks. He may look at the passenger briefly or for four or five seconds before returning his gaze to the front. Some of these drivers will subconsciously turn the steering wheel slightly to the right when turning to speak. The vehicle will move to the right and then return to the center of the lane once his gaze does likewise. His recognition of, and reaction to, any hazard to the front will be delayed by the length of time of his speaking. This driver is not much use to you to warn you of possible hazards in the roadway. Do not use him for a pilot vehicle.

The "I'm too Important, Lazy, or Busy to Signal" Driver
This guy is just too plain inconsiderate to be out in public. Failing to signal might seem like a minor infraction and maybe it is if there are no other drivers nearby. But when he is in traffic he is a hazard. You don't know what he is going to do or when he is going to do it. That makes him an unnecessary risk. The key word is unnecessary. He is adding to the dangers already out there for no good reason. He knows what he wants to do, where he wants to go and when. He doesn't care that you don't. One study concluded that about 25% of drivers observed didn't signal turns while 50% didn't signal lane changes. Where I live in north Idaho this figure is too high. Most everyone does signal lane changes and turns. I always assume that a driver that doesn't signal will ignore other rules of the road as well. Stay away from this guy. Be extra careful if you are passing him in an adjoining lane.

Angry Driver – This guy is described as having "road rage". You have heard about this. You don't need to analyze why another driver seems to be annoyed, aggravated, angry or out of control. If he cuts you off, you may feel the need to cut him off in return. Don't do it. Don't do anything that will make the situation worse. Avoid eye contact as he may take that as a challenge. What you need to do is to stay calm and get out of his way.

Zombie Driver – You will occasionally encounter these folks on limited-access highways. Asleep at the wheel might also describe him. He appears to be oblivious to other traffic. How do you spot a zombie driver? A zombie driver will select a speed and then stay at that speed no matter what the traffic around him is doing. Generally, it is a speed slightly below the average speed of traffic around him. He will slowly fall behind. He will stay in his lane and generally not make any sudden moves. He might be on cruise control. Not keeping up with the flow of traffic is a tip off. If a driver isn't reacting to the movement of other vehicles, and you haven't noticed any obvious reason for his inattention, assume he is a zombie driver.

When there are two zombie drivers in adjacent lanes, near one another, they will cause the traffic to bunch up behind them. Traffic will build up waiting for a chance to pass. You may even see more than one of these "packs" of traffic, perhaps one quarter mile apart or so. When you see this, what do you suppose you should do? Easy. Just stay between the packs. Eventually they will disperse.

A zombie driver is a hazard to himself and to others. His perception time of, and reaction to, any unexpected occurrence, will be delayed. Then when he finally sees the problem he may, and probably will, overreact. The zombie is another driver to distance yourself from.

The "I Only Plan 50 Feet Ahead" Driver – This is one of the most common hazards you will encounter on limited-access highways. He will drive at various speeds and will also change lanes. His problem, and occasionally yours, is that he appears unable to plan ahead more than about 50 feet. It is as if he can't see very far and is constantly surprised that, suddenly, there is another vehicle in front of him. He will drive a bit faster than the traffic in his lane and then, when just a few feet from the vehicle in front, will either brake suddenly or change lanes, perhaps both. He will often not signal lane changes, as the need for them always seems to come as a last-minute surprise. Like the Hotdog, he is easy to spot and therefore easy to avoid.

As in all situations that pose a hazard to you, ask yourself, "What is the safest way to handle this?" With bad drivers, it is to distance yourself from them. The key is to recognize them. Once you do that, you can avoid them.

Chapter 9

DEFENSIVE DRIVING – THE KEY
TO SURVIVAL

OTHER VEHICLES AND DRIVERS need to be considered as a major part of defensive driving. That's not the end of it though. There are techniques you can develop that will make you an accomplished defensive driver. We will address **Inattentional Blindness** – not consciously realizing all of what you are seeing. We will talk about **Spatial Awareness** – knowing what vehicles and other potential hazards are in your "bubble". We will discuss **"What If"** - how to avoid potentially deadly situations. We will look at **Anticipation** – anticipating other drivers' moves. We will also address **Visualization** – practicing for emergencies without having to experience them. Let's get started.

INATTENTIONAL BLINDNESS

Inattentional blindness is a psychological lack of awareness. It is not a vision problem or another physical fault. It describes something we "see" but do not consciously recognize. When you look at something, for example, the

151

forward view out of your windshield, your eyes "see" everything. The trees, the sky with all its clouds and shading, the grass along the roadway, weeds, flowers, the ditch on either side, and the fences and the trees beyond. Add to that, all of the roadway, road signs, other vehicles, what they are all doing and then any persons on bicycles and animals. Imagine taking a picture of that scene, looking at that picture and thinking about everything in it. How long would that take you?

Now imagine taking another picture an instant later. How long would it take you to once again notice all the items in the picture, and to look for any differences between the first and second pictures? Now also add to all that information whatever sounds you heard during those two pictures. This is what your subconscious is dealing with many times a second.

If all this information were forwarded to your conscious brain, your consciousness would be so overloaded that you would be unable to function. Instead of forwarding all that information, your subconscious steps in to make sense of the myriad of stimuli. It sorts through all of it, ignores what it believes irrelevant, and forwards just the important information that you need at that time. If your subconscious has been trained properly, it will forward all possible hazards to you. It will ignore what it is unimportant for the task at hand.

One study of Inattentional Blindness is known as the Invisible Gorilla test. College students were asked to watch a short video of two teams, dressed differently, passing a basketball around. The students were told to either count the number of passes by one team, or to count bounce passes vs. aerial passes. In one version of the video, a woman with an umbrella walked through the scene. In another, a person wearing a gorilla suit walked through. The students were not told there would be a woman or a gorilla in the video. They were told to look for the basketballs. Afterwards the students were asked if they noticed anything unusual in the basketball scenes. Fifty percent did not report seeing either the woman or the gorilla. The students trained their brains to look for the basketball passes or bounces. Do you suppose their failure to "see" the woman or the gorilla was a result of their subconscious deciding that information was irrelevant to the task at hand?

How does your subconscious know what stimuli is important to you at any time, so that it can forward all the relevant information? It is up to you to train it. By teaching it what is important for the task at hand. How?

Let's look at two scenarios. In the first you are a passenger in a vehicle and are helping the driver to navigate to find your destination. You are looking for a specific farm. You consciously think, "Where is that red barn on the right, at the intersection of route 22? After I see that, the correct turn-off is the third one on the right." You are training your brain to look for the barn and for the correct roadway turnoff. You are not concerned about traffic or road hazards; the driver is doing that. You may well see them but it isn't what you trained your subconscious to look for. The important stimuli for your subconscious to forward concerns finding the farm, not driving hazards. In the second scenario, you are the driver. You think, "Well, I need to look out for other vehicles, including motorcycles, bicycles and pedestrians in the roadway. I also need to be aware of the road conditions, roadside hazards and signs." You may not consciously "see" the correct barn or the correct road to the farm. Your passenger has been assigned that role. Your passenger will let you know where to turn. See the difference?

Have you ever heard someone explain an auto accident by saying he never saw whatever it was that he hit? If not, you will. Talk with any officer that has experience investigating auto accidents. He or she will tell you a failure to "see" motorcyclists, even in broad daylight, is common. A distraction is always a possible reason but it may well have been inattentional blindness. If the driver wasn't looking for motorcycles, only cars and trucks, he wouldn't have consciously "seen" the motorcycle. The driver did see the motorcycle but his subconscious didn't know it was important. It didn't forward that information. You need to consciously look for all vehicles and other hazards that may occur on the roadways. This way your subconscious learns what is important and will forward that information to your consciousness. Remember when you first started driving and it took all your concentration to stay in the center of your lane? After a while your subconscious took over this routine part of driving. You could then concentrate on possible hazards and other matters of driving. You no longer had to consciously think "stay just a foot or so to the left of the center of the roadway". You no longer must consciously think "move my right foot to the brake" when the need to brake arises. Your foot will automatically be on the pedal without conscious thought. When your subconscious is properly trained, it will look for all the normal, potential hazards without the need for your constant attention. When one pops up it will let you "see" it. Your subconscious will forward the routine, possible hazards out there. Your conscious mind will be able to focus on the unexpected or unusual hazards.

SPATIAL AWARENESS – YOUR PERSONAL "BUBBLE"

Spatial awareness means being aware of all other vehicles and objects within the area around you. You should be aware of all vehicles, pedestrians, animals, road conditions, and any other potential hazard. You don't have to look directly at these objects. You just need to train your brain to pay attention to include them. When your subconscious is properly trained, it will let you know when a common, potential hazard appears. You will automatically look at it and take the appropriate action. This leaves your conscious mind free to watch for unexpected hazards.

Imagine that you are driving on a two-lane roadway, one lane in each direction. You are in the country. Now imagine looking down on your vehicle from a bird's eye view. Imagine an oblong, sort of circle, with most of it in front of you. The front of it will extend as far as you can see. Included within this circle is the lane on the left, both road shoulders, and a bit of the bushes, trees and fields. Just a little way, where animals might come from. Now extend the circle behind you to include any vehicles approaching from that direction. This is your "bubble".

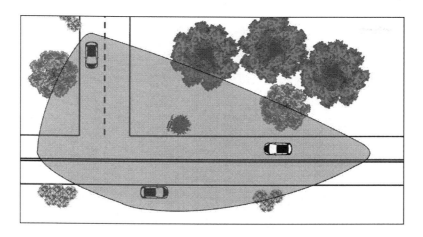

Nothing enters it without your knowledge. Anything that can create a hazard to you is within your conscious view.

This bubble is not just two dimensional. You also need to be aware of some altitude above you. You need to be aware of overhead signs, whether along the roadway shoulders or overhead.

Once, while driving with my wife, we saw a small plane crash into the roadway in front of us. The weather was close to freezing. It was raining lightly. We had seen the plane circling off to our right. It descended in a slow spiral where there was only a farmer's field, no airport. It disappeared off to our right behind some trees. We slowed, as it appeared that it was going to come down somewhere near, soon. Suddenly, it reappeared on the right, just a few feet

> *off the ground. It looked like it was going to cross directly in front of us. A guard rail on the right sheared off the landing gear and the plane came to rest on the roadway, about 30 yards in front of us. The wings had iced up and there was about an inch or so on the windshield. Fortunately, the two folks inside received only minor injuries.*

I am not suggesting that you need to include all air traffic in your bubble. Just include enough altitude in your bubble that seems to make sense at the time.

Your bubble will constantly be changing shape as the conditions warrant. Imagine you are driving on a narrow street in town. There is one lane each way and vehicles are parked on both sides of the road. Businesses line the sides. San Luis Obispo in California comes to mind. It is a vibrant college town with a lot of pedestrian traffic on and around the streets. Students are riding bicycles about. The streets are crowded and parking spaces fill quickly.

As you drive through town, your bubble will be much smaller than on the highway, as traffic moves much slower. However, you will include in your bubble all parked vehicles and even the sidewalks beyond. Is anyone about to step out of a driver's door into your lane? Is any vehicle about to pull out? Are there any brake lights on that might indicate either of the foregoing? Any dogs or children at intersections or about to come from between parked vehicles? You will eventually "see" these things without conscious thought. You just need to train your brain to look for them. That brings us to the next section.

ANTICIPATION

This section will be an interesting challenge for you. You now know that your teen brain isn't fully developed yet. That portion of your brain that allows you to imagine possible future scenarios isn't at its best yet. Nevertheless, being able to imagine possible future problems will be a great help in remaining safe when driving. So, let's give your teen brain some practice.

When you are driving, you know where you want to go and what you need to do next to get there. It would be helpful, and safer, if you also knew what other drivers around you were going to do. Imagine driving on a freeway when a car in the next lane over, just a few seconds ahead, was going to move into your lane. Suppose you knew that even though he hasn't signaled. How would you know that? Sometimes it isn't that difficult to do. You just must look a bit ahead of the other vehicle to see what the driver sees, or should see. Then you can anticipate what it is that he is likely to do. Here are some examples:

Right Lane Exit Only – Imagine driving on a limited-access highway and you are in the center of three lanes in your direction. You see a sign in the shoulder that says "Right lane exit only". That means the right lane will end with the exit. There is a vehicle in that lane just one or two car lengths ahead of you. It does not have any turn signal on. Is it going to exit? Is it going to move into your lane at the last possible instant? What is the safest way to handle this? If your speed is a little faster than his, slow down. Assume he will enter your lane and give him room to do so. If he exits, you will have lost only one or two seconds but you will have remained safe. If he moves into your lane at the last possible second, you will have anticipated it and remained safe, despite his poor driving.

Drifting Vehicle – If you see a vehicle in front of you one lane over, and it is drifting slightly towards your lane, there is a good chance it will move into your lane, with or without a signal. If you see traffic backed up in the next lane over you can anticipate that some traffic in that lane will move into yours. Anticipating what other vehicles ahead of you will do isn't always all that difficult. Just pay attention to what the traffic in the lanes over from you should be seeing. Then you will know what they might do.

Stopped Vehicle on Shoulder of Multi-Lane Highway – Imagine that you are driving in the second lane from the right and you see a vehicle on the right shoulder up ahead, about a quarter mile. There is a tractor-trailer in the right lane about one or two seconds ahead of you. Tractor-trailer drivers will, almost always, move out of the right lane as they pass any vehicle on the shoulder, whether or not there are people around it. Expect that the tractor-trailer will move into your lane. Slow down to allow him to do so. Slowing down lets him know you see him and will allow him room to enter your lane. He will return to the right lane after passing the stopped vehicle. Some folks other than tractor-trailer drivers will also move out of the right lane in these situations. You should also, especially if there are people around the stopped vehicle.

Another Situation with A Tractor-trailer – Imagine you are again in the center lane of three lanes, of a six-lane, limited-access highway, with a large, grassy median. Traffic is moderate. There is a tractor-trailer up ahead in the right lane. As you are traveling faster than it is, you will be even with it shortly. There is a car in the lane behind the tractor-trailer, slowly gaining on it. It will catch up to the tractor-trailer about the same time you do. The driver must either slow down or move into your lane to avoid an accident. As you continue driving, that car doesn't change speed nor does it signal a lane change. What do you do?

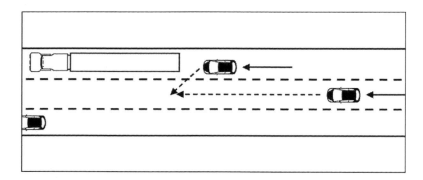

You do what you should always do when confronted with a choice when driving – you will choose the safest alternative. Assume he will pull into your lane at the last possible moment, with or without signaling. This would be an example of the "I only plan 50 feet ahead" driver. Either slow down and give the car safe room to enter your lane or move into the lane to your left. You will encounter this situation often on limited-access highways. Many times, there will be no lane change signal. The vehicle will simply move into your lane at the last possible moment.

Debris in Roadway – You see a tire tread lying in the roadway in the lane to your right. There is a vehicle in that lane. Expect that vehicle to move out of his lane. He may move into yours, or if there is room, in the other direction. He may do so without signaling. Assume he will move into your lane and allow him room by slowing down or move another lane to the left. If he does stay in his lane and runs over the tread, it may be flipped into your lane. Best to be far away from it. Any debris in the roadway can cause damage to your vehicle and can affect control.

Driver Looks Over His Shoulder Towards Your Vehicle
Imagine driving on a multi-lane highway with moderate to heavy traffic. There is a vehicle one or two car lengths ahead in the lane to your right. The driver looks over his left shoulder in your direction and moves his vehicle a little bit left. He is probably going to move into your lane. Drive accordingly. Sometimes you will notice a driver in the lane to your left, look over his right shoulder at your vehicle. He may also be drifting towards your lane. You should also expect that he will move into your lane.

Just recently I was driving in town in heavy traffic. I was behind a tractor-trailer that had a supermarket logo on the rear. There was a supermarket up ahead on the right. The driver started to slow down and move left as if to change lanes, but he didn't signal. Was he going to move left? I wanted to make a right turn at the upcoming intersection and I was tempted to move to the right of the tractor-trailer. But I

> *guessed that he might be headed to the super market.*
> *As it turned out, he was preparing to make a right*
> *turn into the supermarket driveway but only signaled*
> *as he began his right turn. He had moved left before*
> *making the right turn to allow himself room to make*
> *the tight right turn. Anticipating that he might turn*
> *right helped me avoid a possible accident.*

There are many hints out there about when other drivers might move into your lane. Look ahead of other vehicles as well as your own. By anticipating what the driver in front or in the next lane over might do, you will be well on your way to becoming an accomplished defensive driver.

WHAT IF

This section concerns driving scenarios that are "Low Occurrence/High Risk". This is a term used in police training to plan for dangerous situations before they occur. They may not occur often but when they do, they pose a great risk of harm. This low occurrence/high risk way of thinking will help to keep you safe. Perhaps the most common low occurrence/high risk situation would be the possibility of a head-on crash. The chance of it occurring is slim but, if it does happen, the outcome can easily result in serious injury or death. A great way to avoid these possible outcomes is to practice "what if".

Imagine that you are driving on a two-lane roadway, one in each direction, separated only by a center lane marker. You see a car approaching from the opposite direction. Two vehicles, approaching each other at 55 miles an hour or so, and passing within a few feet of each other, pose a serious, potential hazard. You should be thinking - "what if" he comes over the center line into my lane? If you are each traveling at 55 miles an hour, the distance between you and the other vehicle is closing at about 165 feet a second. The distance between your two vehicles will lessen by the length of a soccer field in two seconds. Not much time to decide what to do. What should you do if he does come into your lane? You should be looking for an escape path anytime there is a "High Risk" situation. An approaching vehicle, on a two-lane roadway, is a serious, potential hazard. Is there a wide shoulder? A field beyond? What is the best option for you in that scenario? Practice this "what if" scenario as you drive. Train yourself to always look for an out in situations that are high risk, such as head-on traffic. After a while you will do this automatically, within a fraction of a second, with little conscious thought.

Another less scary scenario involves an animal in the roadway. This should be a "low occurrence/low risk" situation but you could turn it into a "high-risk" situation by the wrong driving tactic. A natural reaction to seeing an animal crossing the roadway would be to brake and turn completely out of its way. But as you now know, you can only make small steering wheel adjustments at highway driving speeds or you risk loss of control and a possible rollover. You will do your best to avoid the animal but sometimes you may not be able to do so. When driving in areas where animals might appear, it is good insurance to drive a bit more slowly anyway. By imagining this scenario when in the countryside you will only make small steering adjustments when an animal appears in front of you. By imagining this scenario, you will train your subconscious to react accordingly. You won't panic and automatically make quick, large steering adjustments

As long as we are talking about animals in the roadway here is a tip about deer crossing in the roadway. If a deer crosses, stops off the roadway and looks back, it is probably looking for its young ones or another deer. That other deer may well try to cross as you approach, especially if it is a young one. Always slow down and look for other deer. Where you see one there are probably more nearby. This might apply to other animals as well but I have seen it often with deer.

Another category of "what if" to practice concerns your vehicle. Modern vehicles are getting more reliable with each year. You may drive many years and not experience a flat tire, a stuck accelerator or a brake failure. Tires rarely fail if they are properly maintained. I have had only one brake failure, and that was 54 years ago. But there were some recent problems with certain new vehicles having acceleration problems. The vehicle would accelerate fully, with no input from the driver, as if the driver floored the gas pedal. When you hear problems like this occurring, ask yourself what you would do. If you don't know how to handle the problem, research it online, or ask a trusted person for advice. In the stuck acceleration situation, you might think to shut off the ignition. In most vehicles, you would lose power steering and braking. The steering wheel might even lock up. Not a good time to learn that shifting into neutral and braking would be a far better choice. Once stopped in a safe area, you could shut the ignition off.

Sometimes you will only have a choice between a "bad" option and a "not as bad" option when practicing "what if". Sounds scary, doesn't it? Driving can be scary sometimes. But you don't want to "freeze" in such a situation. By practicing "what if" you will be prepared to take appropriate action in any situation you can imagine. You won't lose precious time trying to decide what to do, or worse, by freezing and taking no action at all.

VISUALIZATION

Whenever you imagine yourself performing an action in the absence of physical action you are using visualization. You may be on your way to compete in a water polo game. You imagine yourself scoring a goal over the other team's best defender. That is visualization. Unlike the "what if" situation in the above section, which is practiced while driving, visualization can be practiced while at home in your favorite chair, your bed or any place you can have a bit of peace and quiet. This way you can prepare for any imagined emergency situation that might occur on the road without the danger of being in that situation. You will be training your brain how to respond, and improving your motor skills, before an actual emergency occurs. This will give you confidence and help to keep you calm when in an actual dangerous situation. Sound too good to be true?

One study conducted by Dr. Biasiotto at the University of Chicago involved three groups of people who were tested on how many basketball free throws they could make. Afterwards, the first group was assigned to practice every day for an hour. The second group was to just visualize making free throws. The third group was told to do neither. After thirty days, they were again tested. Let's take the third group first. As you might expect, they did not improve. The first group improved 24%. Not bad, and probably expected as well. However, the second group improved by 23% without ever touching a basketball! Amazing, isn't it? You can improve yourself in many areas of your life by using visualization. Many professional and Olympic athletes use it. You can too. So how do you apply this to improve your driving skills? This is an example where practicing visualization would have made a life-threatening situation a lot less dangerous.

I was 18 years old and had little experience driving. I had no formal defensive driver training. I was driving about 55 miles an hour on a two-lane roadway in rural Tennessee. The lanes were separated only by a broken line. It was about two a.m. There were grassy shoulders sloping away to forest on both sides. This stretch of roadway was a long straightaway. My brother and a friend were asleep in the back seat. I saw headlights coming towards me from the distance, perhaps six seconds away. It looked like the lights were slightly in my lane. I watched it for a second or so, I guess to be sure. It looked to be coming more into my lane. I flashed my high beams to alert the other driver. Then, in what seemed like an instant, it was fully in my lane. In another second or so we were going to hit head-on. I swerved into the opposite lane, still going about 55 miles an hour. We passed, each in the others' lane. Immediately, after we passed, the other vehicle swerved back into its own lane. The whole situation occurred in just a few seconds. We were lucky. In those days, few cars had seat belts. There were no airbags. We easily could have died that day.

What did I do wrong? Just about everything. First, I never slowed down. Disbelief about what was happening and not knowing what to do caused me to do nothing but flash my high beams and wait for the other driver to respond. I continued to drive at the same speed and did not brake or move onto the shoulder. I had never experienced someone driving towards me into my lane. I had never imagined it. Never gave it any thought. Remember what you learned about being in a threatening situation? Your body goes into a "Freeze, Fight or Flight" mode. I essentially froze when I saw the car in my lane. Only at the last possible second did I take any evasive action. Passing each other in the wrong lanes is a bad idea. And, it was unnecessary if I had reacted appropriately.

What should I have done? I should have been practicing "what if" – looking for an out for just this scenario. I should have immediately applied the brakes when I first saw the headlights and thought the car might be in my lane. I should have planned to drive onto the shoulder when it became necessary. Flashing the headlights was ok but the other driver was probably falling asleep. He did not react to my flashing lights. I wasted time waiting for the other driver to move out of my lane. If I had driven onto the shoulder at 55 miles per hour we might have rolled over. But I had enough time to slow down to a more reasonable speed and could have driven onto the shoulder without much risk of losing control of the car. I hesitated too long before taking any evasive action. Even then, what I did was extremely risky. You don't ever want to pass on the wrong side.

Visualization is an important tool in your defensive driving tool bag. Had I thought about what to do in that situation, before it happened, I would have reacted the way I practiced it in my mind, not the way it turned out. We survived only through pure luck, not my skills.

Let's go back to the "what if" scenarios. First scenario: the two-lane roadway and the approaching driver, such as just described. Let's not just imagine the view of the approaching vehicle. When you practice visualization try to feel the emotion you would have at such a time. You are traveling 55 miles an hour. Imagine the hum of the tires, maybe even rain. Feel your hands gripping the wheel a bit tighter. Now, what is the best way to handle this? Is there any room on the shoulder? Can you drive onto a nearby meadow if necessary? Think positive! You imagine moving the wheel slightly to the right. You know that is all that is needed to move out of your lane when traveling at highway speeds. You apply the brakes, perhaps lightly if that is all that is needed - perhaps locking them up, relying on the anti-lock and skid-control programming to assist you. Imagine staying calm. Now imagine that you have safely passed by the other vehicle and can re-enter the center of your lane. Do not think negatively! You are going to safely make it past that vehicle. Go over this scenario until you feel confident that you can handle that situation. As you learned in the above example with shooting basketball free throws, you will improve your skills and confidence to respond quickly and confidently in that situation, even though it was an imaginary situation. Practicing this scenario using visualization is a lot safer than waiting for the actual on-coming vehicle in your lane and then trying to decide what to do.

Now imagine the second and third scenarios; the animal in the roadway and the stuck accelerator. You know how to handle those. Imagine the scene, feel your emotions and the feel of the wheel. Hear the traffic. Try to use all your senses that you would experience in the actual setting. Over time you will see other potentially dangerous situations. Eventually you will see someone run a red light. Use visualization to practice how to respond to the red-light runner as if you were in his path. Imagine him coming from the right. Then the left. Think of the best way to respond and then train your brain and your motor skills on how to best respond. Any time you see a dangerous situation, whether it is dangerous to you or others, add it to your visualization practice sessions until you are comfortable with responding to it.

STOPPING/AVOIDANCE DISTANCE

You should always be able to see far enough ahead to be able to avoid anything in the roadway. If there is a disabled vehicle or any other hazard in your path, you will need to be far enough back to either stop or avoid it by changing lanes. If you cannot see as far as your stopping/avoidance distance, you are driving too fast. Stay within your stopping/avoidance distance. If your view forward is reduced by the weather, darkness, or because of a winding or hilly roadway you need to adjust your speed to allow time for you to stop within your sight distance. This can be challenging as sometimes traffic will be heavy enough that you cannot see very far forward, not far enough to stop. In those situations, you need to have another lane you can quickly move into to avoid the obstacle.

Here is a real-life situation that occurred in a ranching area not far from where I live. It occurred on a clear afternoon, on a straight stretch of a two lane, rural roadway that ascended a hill and continued straight on down the other side. It is a beautiful area of farms, fields and woodlands. Folks that live there know the roadway and travel it often. Because the roadway is straight, and there are no cross streets for another ½ mile or so in either direction, it appears to be safe to drive the legal limit. Traffic is always light.

A local woman was driving and ascended the hill traveling at about 50 mph. Just as she passed over the top of the hill she saw a bicyclist in the right part of her lane. He was too close for her to move out of the way or brake. She struck him. Her recognition and reaction times used up the distance between her and the bicyclist before she could turn the steering wheel or apply the brakes. Both she and the bicyclist were legally in the roadway. But being legal didn't save that young man. Even though she was driving at or

> *under the legal speed, she over drove her visual distance.*

Always drive within your stopping/avoidance distance. Use the legal speed limit for a guide, not a required speed.

ALWAYS LEAVE YOURSELF AN OUT

Always try to leave yourself an out, someplace to go, other than the lane you are in. Try not to get blocked in by traffic on both sides, traveling at the same speed. You shouldn't remain next to another vehicle, traveling at the same speed, for any extended time. You should always strive to keep some distance between yourself and other vehicles, not just the one in front. Move up or back. Having vehicles on both sides is risky. They would eliminate any chance for you to move out of your lane if a tire tread, a pothole, ice, a disabled vehicle or another hazard appears in your lane.

Imagine driving uphill in the left lane of a four-lane, separated highway and passing a tractor-trailer in the lane to your right. You would be driving between the tractor-trailer and the guardrail. If there is no shoulder between the guardrail and your lane, you could not move over to avoid a hazard in your lane. Avoid these situations whenever possible. In this example, you should anticipate this possible problem and simply avoid it. Just stay in your lane, or move behind the tractor-trailer and wait for a safer place to pass.

CONCLUSION

There is a lot of information in this chapter. A lot to think about. A lot to practice. By now you realize that driving is a very serious matter. It requires your full-time attention to other vehicles and other drivers as well as road and weather conditions. You know that your ability to judge risk is still improving and will get better with time. You should always choose the safer alternative. You will train your subconscious to see potential hazards and forward that information to your consciousness. You will be aware of all potential hazards within your bubble. You will practice "what if" and visualization.

Sometimes, the best decision is to not drive at all. It has been my experience that drunk drivers are most common in the late evening hours, especially Friday and Saturday. Sunday mornings tend to have the least traffic. A great time to practice. Avoiding snow and ice is always a good decision. Avoiding heavy rain is another good idea. And, another super important decision that you can make, is to avoid being a passenger in a vehicle driven by an inexperienced driver.

Many of the teens that have died in traffic accidents were passengers in vehicles driven by other teens.

If you once thought driving would be easy, you now know better. It needn't be stressful however. The more skilled you get at defensive driving, the more relaxed you will be. You will know that, whatever happens, you will respond calmly and safely.

Chapter 10

FOR PARENTS – CHOOSING A VEHICLE

WHAT IF YOU KNEW that your teen would soon have a serious automobile accident? What vehicle will you choose? What are your priorities? What should they be? My purpose in publishing this manual, rather than keeping it for just my family, is to save the lives of teen drivers. It can help them to survive and become accomplished, defensive drivers; to live long enough to enjoy their own grandchildren. By choosing the safest vehicle you can find, you will be doing your part in keeping your teen safe.

Some general concepts for choosing a safer vehicle. When comparing vehicles, keep these in mind.

- ✓ A taller vehicle has better visibility - to see out of and to be seen.
- ✓ A wider wheelbase provides better handling.
- ✓ A longer and wider vehicle will have larger crumple zones.
- ✓ A heavier vehicle provides a better safety margin in a crash with another, lighter vehicle.

✓ A larger crumple zone provides better protection in a crash.

✓ A vehicle with a lower center of gravity provides better handling ability.

✓ Some taller, well-designed vehicles will have better handling abilities than some other vehicles with a lower center of gravity

✓ Bigger side-view mirrors provide a better driver's view.

✓ A white or other light color makes a vehicle more visible to other drivers.

SAFETY FACTORS

Let's look at some specific factors that make one vehicle a safer choice than another.

Crashworthiness

A good place to start your search for a safer vehicle is the NHTSA website. This acronym stands for the National Highway Transportation Safety Administration. It is the federal agency tasked with "reducing deaths, injuries and economic losses resulting from motor vehicle crashes". Their website lists the "crashworthiness" for most vehicles. It is also a good place to check for recalls and defects of specific vehicles. It rates vehicles using a five-star system. It performs frontal crash tests which examine the impact of a head-on crash into a solid wall at 90 degrees. As most vehicle head-on crashes are offset, those test results do not necessarily reflect the crashworthiness of any particular vehicle in a head-on, offset crash. In December of 2015, NHTSA stated it will add frontal offset crash tests. For those vehicles tested before 2016 the frontal offset test results for older vehicles won't be available.

This website does have a lot of great information on research, safety, driving tips and recalls of various vehicles. Before buying any vehicle, check for the recalls and problems with it on this website.

The Insurance Institute for Highway Safety (IIHS) also has a website which lists the results for the crash simulations they conduct. IIHS rates a vehicle's crashworthiness as either Poor, Marginal, Acceptable or Good. It also rates, on a sliding scale, frontal crash results.

There are some differences in the tests that these two organizations conduct so it is a good idea to research both. IIHS tests crashworthiness in an offset head-on crash which exposes 40% of the front of the vehicle to the impact. More recently IIHS began using a 25% frontal offset crash. It is a more severe test of a vehicle's crashworthiness. These offset tests more closely reflect an actual head-on accident than the straight-on crash. In some cases, while NHTSA gave a five-star rating in a frontal crash to several vehicles, IIHS rated the same vehicles as poor. So, it is a good idea to check both websites before making a selection.

The crash simulations of these two organizations, as good as they are, do not replicate actual collisions between two vehicles. They are good tests of a vehicle crash into a solid, immovable object. They are a great comparison of vehicles in those settings and therefore give a good idea for comparing one against another. But they can be misleading.

A small, light car might get the same crash rating as another, much larger, heavier vehicle. But in a crash between the two, occupants in the larger, heavier vehicle will have a better chance of survival. Actual head-on accidents occur when two vehicles of different weights, size and design, traveling at different speeds, impact each other. It would be impractical, and perhaps impossible, to replicate these situations, given the thousands of combinations possible. Yet, accidents between two vehicles of unequal speed, weight, size and design occur daily.

Crashworthiness ratings do not provide the information needed to determine which of two vehicles would fare the best in an accident between them. Let's look at some of the differences between vehicles, as they relate to their crashworthiness.

Weight

Kinetic energy is the amount of energy needed to decelerate a moving vehicle to a stop. It is also the amount of energy to get a vehicle up to a certain speed. Here, we are concerned only with the energy expended when decelerating in a crash. Imagine a straight, head-on accident between two vehicles. Each is traveling 50 miles an hour. The first weighs 5,000 lbs., about the weight of a full-sized vehicle. The smaller one weighs 2,500 lbs. This would not be the lightest passenger vehicle, but compact vehicles fit in this category. Let's assume that both vehicles have the same safety ratings by the above organizations. Will one vehicle offer better protection than the other?

The higher the kinetic energy, the more energy needed to stop the forward motion of each vehicle. The less the kinetic energy a vehicle has, the less energy needed to stop the forward motion. Makes sense, right? The formula for kinetic energy is one-half the mass times velocity squared. So, for the 5,000-pound vehicle we have half the weight (2,500), times the velocity squared (2,500), giving us 6,250,000 joules, the standard unit of measurement for kinetic energy. Using the same formula, the lighter vehicle will have 3,125,000 joules.

Now, let's figure out what happens to each vehicle when they meet in a straight, head-on crash. For each vehicle to stop its forward motion, it must use up its kinetic energy. In this scenario, some of that energy is absorbed by the "crumple zone" of each vehicle. The crumple zone is that portion of the vehicle designed to collapse before the passenger compartment is compromised. A vehicle with a better crumple zone will absorb more kinetic energy than one with an inferior one. What happens when there is no more crumple zone to absorb energy? The passenger compartment gets compromised.

Let's see what happens in our scenario. As the vehicles crash together they won't stop their forward motion until there is no more kinetic energy left in one of the vehicles. In this example, the lighter vehicle will lose all its forward momentum when its remaining joules are dissipated. It will stop. At this point each vehicle will have used up 3,125,000 joules, the energy of the lighter vehicle. However, the heavier vehicle will still have 3,125,000 joules of kinetic energy left. What happens now?

The heavier vehicle continues forward, using up its remaining energy pushing the lighter vehicle backwards until all its energy is dissipated. The result is that the heavier vehicle decelerates from 50 miles an hour forward, to a lesser speed forward, perhaps 20 or so miles an hour. The lighter vehicle doesn't fare near as well. It decelerates from

50 miles an hour to 0, and then travels backwards at 20 miles an hour. All of this occurs within a few thousandths of a second. In this example, the impact for the heavier vehicle would be approximately the same as hitting an immovable wall at 30 miles an hour. It continued forward at 20 miles an hour after impact. The lighter vehicle would have the equivalent impact of hitting the same wall at 70 miles an hour, forward at 50 miles an hour and instantly backwards at 20. In which vehicle, would you rather be?

This is a hypothetical example, and the numbers given are for explanation purposes. In an actual accident, the amount of kinetic energy dissipated by each vehicle might be different. But the result would still be that the heavier vehicle will continue to move forward after the impact and the lighter one would move backwards. Occupants in the lighter vehicle would have suffered a greater impact than the heavier.

What happens when two vehicles collide on an angle, not straight on? As well as having more kinetic energy, a heavier vehicle will have more momentum than a lighter one traveling at the same speed. Momentum can be calculated as mass (weight) times velocity. It stands to reason that the heavier vehicle will have greater momentum. The more the momentum, the more the resistance to change in direction.

When two vehicles of different weights collide, the heavier vehicle will have more momentum to continue in the direction it was headed. The lighter one will "bounce off" in whatever direction physics dictates. It will have a greater chance of leaving the roadway or into the path of another vehicle.

Many improvements have been made in vehicle safety in the last 20 years. But the laws of physics remain the same. Weight of a vehicle isn't the only factor when considering the crashworthiness of a vehicle, but it is an extremely important one. Imagine a car being hit head-on by a train. Wouldn't you want your teen to be in the train rather than the car? Bigger and heavier counts for a lot in multiple vehicle accidents.

Crumple zones

There is a good reason to consider the size of a vehicle other than for how many occupants will fit within. As a rule, the longer and wider a vehicle, the larger the crumple zones. Crumple zones are designed to absorb the energy of an impact in a traffic accident. They do this through the controlled deformation of various structural components outside of the passenger compartment. Crumple zones are designed to prevent, or at least minimize, intrusion into the passenger compartment. Varying factors make the crumple zone on one vehicle better than another. Design is important. Here is a real-life example of where a well-designed vehicle impacted another vehicle of similar size with much poorer design for safety.

> *When I lived in Arizona, a drunk driver crossed the center line of a city street and hit another sedan head on. The drunk survived with few injuries while the two people in the other vehicle were killed. The primary difference was the superior safety design of the first. It contained almost all the energy from the crash within its crumple zone. There was no appreciable entry into the passenger compartment. In the other vehicle, the front of the car was pushed into the passenger compartment, crushing the occupants. As you might imagine, the better designed vehicle cost about twice as much as the cheaper.*

Larger vehicles have more distance between the passenger compartment and the exterior dimensions. Doors are thicker, hoods are longer and trunk space is greater. It makes sense that there would be a more effective crumple zone in a larger vehicle than in a smaller one. The more structural components there are protecting the front, sides and rear of the passenger compartment, the more kinetic energy that will be absorbed before the passenger compartment is compromised. Few manufacturers tout crumple zones. It may even be close to impossible to compare vehicles in this manner. Rely instead on the tests done by NHTSA, IIHS and any other crash test data you can find. A larger vehicle will generally have larger crumple zones than a smaller one. All other factors being equal, a larger vehicle will be safer.

ELECTRONIC SAFETY FEATURES

Look for the latest electronic safety features. ABS and VSC should be a minimum for any vehicle you select. Manufacturers are continually coming out with new safety features such as front collision warnings and avoidance, pedestrian detection and lane departure warnings. Try for the latest and best of them. It is a good investment in your child's safety.

OVERALL SIZE

Height of a vehicle is important in judging a vehicle's safety. Imagine an intersection accident where a vehicle entering from your left runs into your driver's door. Now imagine you are in a small, low to the ground, car while the other vehicle is a full-sized pickup truck. When the pickup crashes into your door where is the bumper of the pickup in relation to your head? Your torso? In all likelihood, it is in line with your head or upper torso. This is where much of the force impacting your car will occur. Not a good thing. Now imagine that you are in the same pickup and a small car crashes into your driver's door. Where will the car's bumper impact your truck? Probably about where your feet or lower legs are. In which vehicle would you rather be? Even if there is intrusion into your passenger compartment by the other vehicle you are much more likely to survive, with less serious injuries, in the higher vehicle. The location of the point of impact is a major factor in the survivability of a side impact

One argument raised about the safety of higher vehicles is that they can roll over easier than those built lower to the ground. This is a general rule based upon the probable center of gravity of the taller vehicle. But it doesn't allow for vehicle design and handling. A well-designed, full-sized car, truck or SUV will have good, if not great, handling characteristics. Because one vehicle is taller than another isn't necessarily an indication of a greater rollover risk.

I have driven high performance police vehicles at ludicrous speeds (for those days), and standard cars and trucks, at more reasonable speeds, for a lot of years. I have yet to roll one over. The risk of a rollover for any good driver is very small. A rollover is generally caused by the driver's actions, not by that of another driver. There is a much greater chance of your teen being in an accident with another vehicle than causing a rollover. As your teen becomes a good defensive driver, her risk of causing a rollover is very small but other drivers will put her at risk of a crash. She cannot control the actions of other drivers. But you can choose a vehicle that will give her the best protection possible in a crash caused by other drivers.

Another factor that makes a side impact so dangerous is momentum. The vehicle being struck will receive all the other vehicle's energy without having any energy to offset the impact. This is because it is not moving towards the other vehicle. This type of accident is extremely deadly for the occupants of the vehicle being struck in the side. There is not much of a crumple zone in the side of a vehicle. Likely, there will be intrusion into the passenger compartment. The best-case scenario would be intrusion below the head and torso. The taller vehicle provides the better margin of safety.

Another safety benefit of a larger vehicle is the size of the side mirrors. Small vehicles generally have smaller mirrors which will not provide the view of larger ones. With larger mirrors, you will see more of the lanes to your sides and the vehicles in them. A driver should be able to see the complete width of the lanes to the left and right, not just part of each. When the view of an approaching vehicle leaves the rear-view mirror, it should be visible in the side mirror. There should be no gap where the driver cannot see the vehicle. If there is, the mirrors are too small.

Manufacturers seem more concerned about style than safety in designing side view mirrors. Some are even cut down to small triangles. Compare the size of mirrors found on compact cars with those on pickup trucks and tractor-trailers. Their size should be dictated by need, not style. If trucks need large mirrors, and tractor-trailers need even larger mirrors why don't compact cars? Seems to me compact vehicles should have the largest mirrors, as occupants of them are at greatest risk of injury and death. They need the best possible view of all other traffic. Pick a vehicle with adequate mirrors.

VISIBILITY – SEE AND BE SEEN

We talked about seeing and being aware of all possible hazards within your bubble. You know that you need to see the traffic, roadway and potential hazards to the front. When driving in traffic that is close together, this isn't always possible. But it should be your constant goal. Move back or move over to improve your view to the front. One easy way to have a good view is to have a taller vehicle than most others. A full-sized suv or pickup truck fits the bill here.

Another benefit of a taller vehicle is that you are more visible to other drivers. And while we are on this subject, what color vehicle is the most visible to others? Other than possibly the lime green of fire trucks, white is the easiest to see. Well, maybe not in a snowstorm, but you shouldn't be driving in a snowstorm anyway. When driving at dawn and dusk, a lighter vehicle is easier to see than a darker one. Newer vehicles have running lights that are on all the time. This makes the car more visible to the front. But some, perhaps most, vehicles with running lights don't have any running lights to the rear or the side. A lighter color makes it easier for others to see you.

HANDLING CHARACTERISTICS

When I first started driving, most cars had soft suspension. When going over a bump, the car would travel up and down which softened the ride. It would continue to move up and down a few times after the bump. This comfort came at a cost. When cornering, the car would lean to the outside of the turn. When the turn was completed, it would sort of swing back side-to-side into an upright position. Not a good suspension if the need for a fast maneuver became necessary. Vehicles today have a lot better suspension systems and handle bumps and turns without the rocking around from past years. Having said that, there are some vehicles that handle turns and stopping a lot better than others, even in the same price range.

Take any potential vehicle purchase out for a test drive. Test it for maximum braking and cornering. Tell the sales person that he should buckle up because you are going to test the handling capabilities of the vehicle. Slam on the brakes from about 25 miles an hour. Brake hard again at 50 or so. It should stop quickly with little front end dip. Make rapid left and right wheel corrections. There should be minimum body roll. Of course, perform these tests in an empty parking lot or street where there is no traffic.

> *I once heard a comedian tell a story about test driving a car. He told the salesman to buckle up as he wanted to try something he had seen in a cartoon. I was in the market for a new car anyway so I decided to try that comment on a car salesman. I said that to one when he failed to fasten his seat belt. He looked surprised and scared at the same time, hurriedly buckled up, but didn't say anything. I guess hoping to make the sale was more important than risking a crash. No, I didn't do any cartoon maneuvers but I kind of wish I had.*

RELIABILITY

There are websites that rate motor vehicles for reliability. Generally, you can find results going back several years for each model and year. If a vehicle has had problems with steering, brakes, or electronic control systems you want to know about it. Has it had any problem which resulted in a recall? It is easy to find information on any recalls for a vehicle. There are several websites that provide this information. NHTSA is one. If the vehicle has had a recall, you will want to know if the vehicle has been updated. The current owner should have the paperwork showing any updates. Any dealer for that vehicle model should be able to look up the update records for the vehicle.

Recalls are not uncommon and not necessarily a reason to decide against a vehicle. A more important factor to look for is whether the manufacturer voluntarily made the recalls as soon as the problems were found, or did it delay until the federal government, or public pressure, forced them to do it? Recalls about non-safety issues are not a real concern unless the manufacturer has a reputation for delaying recalls. That is a red flag. This information can also be found on the internet.

AGE

As a rule, a newer vehicle should have fewer mechanical problems than an older one. But a well-maintained vehicle, especially one with lower mileage, can be just as reliable as a newer one, perhaps even better. It is worth a few dollars to have an independent mechanic check out a potential purchase for problems. You should also be able to check the service records of any used vehicle. If there are none, you might want to pass on that purchase.

COST

Unless you have unlimited funds, cost will enter any consideration about purchasing a vehicle. The extra cost to buy a safer vehicle will buy insurance that no company can provide – insurance to protect your son or daughter. You can always buy an older vehicle with better safety features than a newer one with fewer, for the same money.

GAS MILEAGE

This is something that our government has been promoting for a long time. Lots of folks have joined on this bandwagon for various reasons – "saving the planet" is one. As a result, our cars have gotten smaller and lighter. Smaller and lighter, as you now know, means less safe. Recent studies have shown what should be obvious. You have a greater risk of serious injury and death in a smaller, lighter vehicle. Buying a smaller vehicle to save on gas, or electric power, is a mistake. A bad one. I have published this manual to share my knowledge about keeping your teen safe – not about saving gasoline. Your goal should be to give your child the absolute best chance of surviving any traffic accident. The additional cost for buying a little more gasoline buys you the extra insurance for saving your child's life. There are plenty of other ways you can save the planet without sacrificing your teen's safety in the process.

STYLE

We all want a stylish car or truck. Your teen will want something that her friends will say is "cool". Something he or she can show off. That is to be expected. You may even be able to find such a vehicle, with all the above features, in your price range. That would be great. But I put this criterion last because it does nothing to keep your child safe. The first vehicle we bought for our first son was a used, full-sized, four-wheel drive pickup. Our second son was given a well-traveled, older Cadillac Fleetwood Brogham. Neither of these broke the bank, yet both fit the above criteria. The truck did look cool but I was concerned that the giant Caddy would embarrass our son when driving to school. Looking out the windshield from the front seat looked like we were in a boat. My concern was unfounded as he was happy just to have a vehicle. If he ever took any ribbing about it at school, we never heard about it.

CONCLUSION

The leading cause of death among driving-age teens is traffic accidents. What are the odds of your child having an accident in the next few years? What vehicle would you pick if you knew your child was going to be in a serious vehicle accident? You cannot guarantee that your child won't be in an accident. What you can do is guarantee that she has been given the absolute best chance of surviving a serious accident, with few or no injuries. There are many decisions you have made, and will make, concerning your teen. Choosing his or her first vehicle is one of the most important you will ever make.

Automobile accidents don't always happen to someone else. The odds are that you know of someone, maybe even someone in your family, who has been in a serious vehicle accident, maybe even a fatality. Remember what you have learned about the teen brain? Your child's ability to judge risk isn't as good as yours and it won't be until she is 25 or so. Use your more mature judgment to choose your teen's first vehicle. Make it the safest possible.

Chapter 11

CARJACKING AND ABDUCTIONS

DON'T ASSUME it cannot happen to you. It happens daily. I am not an expert on carjacking or on abductions but I can give you a few thoughts. Please follow it up with your own research. A good place to start is the U.S. Department of State website. Look for an article entitled "Carjacking- Don't be a Victim". This site is primarily for traveling out of the country but it has some information that applies anywhere. There are many other websites and books on this subject. Do your homework.

CARJACKING

Carjackers look for opportunity. Some of the places where carjackers might frequent include intersections controlled by traffic lights or signs, public garages, shopping malls, self-serve gas stations, grocery stores, automatic teller machines, and highway entrance and exit ramps. As you can see, pretty much anywhere a carjacker would have access to a stopped vehicle, especially when you are alone, is a potential carjacking location.

"Bump and Rob" is one method of stealing your car which may be considered a version of carjacking. A vehicle bumps you from behind. When you get out to check for damage, an occupant of the other vehicle gets into your vehicle and drives off. If you are involved in this type of accident, look for a public place with lots of folks about where you can stop and discuss the accident. Call 911 or at least the local police number before exiting your vehicle. Meanwhile, keep your doors locked. When you do get out, keep your keys with you.

Common advice to reduce your risk of becoming a carjacking victim includes the following:

Approaching and getting into your vehicle – Stay alert when approaching your vehicle; have your key in hand; look around the vehicle and inside before getting in; don't stop and talk to strangers asking directions or handing out flyers. If there are any other people about, especially if their presence makes you uncomfortable, immediately lock your doors and drive off.

While driving – Keep your doors locked and windows rolled up far enough to prevent someone from reaching inside when you are stopped; when coming to a stop, leave enough room to drive off, if necessary. As you have already learned, when you stop, you should always be far enough behind the vehicle in front to see where the rear tires of that vehicle in front contact the roadway. Preventing a carjacking is another reason why you should do so. Do not stop to assist someone nearby an apparently disabled vehicle unless you know them. Instead, continue and, when safe to do so, stop to call the local police department. They will provide the needed assistance.

Getting out of your vehicle – Park in well-lighted areas; avoid parking next to large vehicles that could have someone within that you cannot see. Examples include windowless vans, motor homes, camping trailers and fifth wheels. Do not leave valuables in plain view which might encourage someone to wait for your return.

Your car can be replaced. Your credit cards, phone, and money can also be replaced. If someone demands your vehicle and that person has a firearm, don't argue. If all he wants is your vehicle, let him have it. However, if it appears that he wants you as well, it is no longer a carjacking but a potential abduction. Your best chance of staying alive is to drive off as fast as possible. Don't open a window to talk to him or open your door. Don't try to talk him out of it. Leave as fast as possible. If you are outside your vehicle, run. You can even throw him the car keys to distract him. One self-defense expert I read about said he carries a 20-dollar bill in his pocket, separate from his wallet. If someone attempted to rob him he would rather throw the 20-dollar bill and run than confront the criminal. His theory is that it is safer and a whole lot less trouble than using a firearm or fighting, even if he believed he would prevail. Your chance of surviving a carjacking/abduction is never going to be better than it is when you are first contacted. Anything you can do that would temporarily distract him will give you a better chance of escaping.

ABDUCTIONS

Large parking garages offer a place, out of the public view, to kidnap or otherwise assault victims. Be especially vigilant when in any location where another person can get to you alone. When parking in a large lot, such as at a movie theater or shopping center, park as close as you can to the entrance of the mall or store. If at night, park under or near an overhead light. Do not park next to any large vehicle that you cannot easily see into. Stay away from any van with no windows or windows that are covered. I like to park away from other vehicles, usually far from the entrance. There is less chance of door dings. But I don't believe that I am at risk of being abducted. The same is not true for teens and college students. Abduction of female college students by serial rapists and assorted criminals is a reality. Every year young girls go missing from, or near, college campuses. Some are never found. Do not think that you are not at risk. The risk may be numerically small, but it is there.

If you are returning from a supermarket, movie theater, sporting event or other public gathering, and you feel uneasy about someone nearby, go back inside and ask for security or someone else to accompany you. If you feel uneasy about some specific person, that is your subconscious telling you there is a reason for it. Your subconscious is capable of picking up on threatening body language you may not consciously recognize. Heed this feeling. Anytime you are returning to your vehicle in a somewhat secluded place, pay attention to your surroundings. Do not talk on your phone or otherwise be distracted. See who else is about who might confront you. Wait for others going to their vehicles so that you won't be alone.

When leaving your car with a parking attendant, leave only the ignition key or remote, no house keys. I rarely use valet parking, or have any reason to give my vehicle key to a parking attendant. But if you are going to do it, remove, or at least hide, any documents that have your residential address. I know - you would usually have insurance and other documents in the vehicle. But if you are leaving your vehicle with some unknown person, for whatever reason, removing the documents is a good idea. When you get to my age, you probably won't be at much risk of being abducted. Meanwhile, while you are of a target age for an abduction, take all precautions possible to prevent it.

SELF DEFENSE TRAINING

I am an advocate of martial arts, boxing, wrestling and any other physical training that will give you confidence in defending yourself. It will help to make you immune from assault and kidnapping.

One of the toughest troopers I knew was our Defensive Tactics Instructor in the New York State Police academy. He was also the smallest trooper I ever met. Generally, we were all six feet or taller. He was five foot, eight and three-quarters inches tall, weighed about 150 pounds, and kept himself in great condition. He was proficient in several martial arts. He could throw even the heaviest opponents onto the ground, using their own weight against them. He made up for his small stature by learning enough of the various martial arts to control even the biggest and most belligerent fighters.

You don't have to be a big person to be able to defend yourself. You don't have to become a black belt in martial arts or a championship boxer or wrestler. You just need to learn enough moves to allow you to prevent another person from taking control of you long enough to get away. Aikido is a form of martial arts that uses the attacker's momentum to throw or control him. It can be very effective and doesn't require you to be bigger or stronger than the assailant. While a police officer needs to control a suspect after the initial encounter, you don't. You just need to prevent him from controlling you long enough for you to escape. Never allow yourself to be taken to a second location by a potential abductor. I highly recommend that you learn enough self-defense techniques so that you are comfortable with being able to defend against an attack long enough to get away.

TOOLS FOR SELF DEFENSE

There are some good self-defense alternatives other than martial arts but you should have them available and in your hand when needed. I still strongly recommend some martial arts training, but there are times that the following alternatives may be of practical use. Electronic stun devices and pepper spray are two self-defense alternatives in common use by police departments. Both can be very effective but both have limitations.

Electronic stun devices – These devices can disable a person immediately. They work by temporarily overpowering the muscles between and near the impact area of the contact points. The electrical charge causes the muscles to contract rather violently, overriding any possible control by the person stunned. Some stun devices fire contact points, two barbed metal points attached to wires. The charge is supplied by an electronic circuit in the "gun" held by the would-be victim. Other electronic stun devices are hand-held which requires that the contact points be placed on the assailant. These tools will work on drunks and others who are under the influence of illegal drugs, even though they are usually indifferent to pain compliance techniques. They will even disable people who display super human strength. I have seen a video of it being used on a steer – knocking it down immediately.

I think it might even be a good defense against bears but I haven't figured out exactly how to test that theory.

Hollywood gets it wrong with its depiction of electronic stun devices. In the movies I have seen, the assailant goes down immediately and then remains incapacitated for some time afterwards. A stun device can disable instantly but, in my experience, the effect lasts only while the electrical pulse is applied. Once the pulsing stops, a person regains muscle control quickly.

Because they are instantly disabling and cause no lasting injuries, it is an excellent tool for self-defense. However, they also have limitations. If it is the type that has two darts connected to wires, both must contact the assailant, and the right distance apart. The distance from the assailant is critical. Too far and one dart will miss. Too close, and there won't be much area impacted by the darts. Heavy clothing can also impair, if not eliminate, its effectiveness.

A common electronic stun device used by many police departments is the Taser. It is the one with which I am most familiar. It is a hand-held device that looks similar to a pistol.

Because I taught at the Mesa, Arizona Police Academy, I had the opportunity to watch hundreds of recruits get tasered. It was a required part of their training. I was tasered as well. It felt like an instant, super strong, vibrating muscle spasm. I immediately fell to the mat, unable to hold myself upright. After the pulsing stopped, I could stand up within a few seconds.

It is a great self-defense tool in trained hands. Some states regulate the possession and use of stun devices. Your state may even ban its use, allowing it only in defense of deadly force. Research the statutes of your state. You should be able to find any laws regarding their possession and use on the internet.

Pepper spray – This can also be an effective defensive tool. But it also has its limitations. It isn't quite as disabling as the electronic stun devices I am familiar with. Pepper spray affects a person's ability to breath and causes the eyes to burn. Its main ingredient is capsaicin, derived from chili peppers. Yes, the edible kind. When sprayed, most persons will bend over and cover their eyes. Bending over makes breathing easier and covering the eyes eases the pain somewhat.

A serious limitation to the use of pepper spray is the dispersion of the spray. We found that the spray worked best if it had a wide pattern rather than a narrow stream. For the hand-held variety, you generally need to be about three to eight feet away. Too close and the spray may not be dispersed enough. Too far and the spray will be too dispersed. It needs to get into the eyes and breathed into the lungs. If there is a breeze coming from either side, the spray may not even reach the assailant. Worse, if the breeze is coming towards you, you will get the spray, not the assailant. If you spray an assailant, and then come in contact with him, you will probably get the spray on yourself. Also, a small percentage of persons aren't affected enough to become disabled.

Over time I witnessed hundreds of police recruits being pepper sprayed. They were required to spray each other at a distance of four or five feet. Just as with the Tasers, it was part of their training. Some were still able to fight, even with their eyes closed. Officers learned that it was a bad idea to get some of the spray on themselves. Wrestling with a person who has been sprayed can easily affect the officer's ability to defend herself. Not a good thing for an officer or for you.

Our police department tracked all uses of pepper spray in actual police/citizen confrontations. It was about 95% effective. The remaining 5% could still fight. Some of the assailants were under the influence of illegal drugs. Certain illegal drugs eliminate the sensation of pain which can reduce the effectiveness of pepper spray.

When pepper spray first became available for police departments, I was an advocate for providing it to all our officers. It was quickly suggested that I be given the honor of testing it. The police chief, a lieutenant and I were selected to be the first "volunteer" test subjects. My breathing became difficult and my eyes burned - a lot! When I forced my eyes open, it felt like someone was poking a stick into them. Hosing me off with cold water helped but it took quite a while before the effects were completely gone.

Pepper spray can be kept in a purse, pocket or vehicle. When you are in a situation where you feel unsafe, have it in your hand. It won't be of much use if you cannot easily access it when needed. Replace the pepper spray every year or so to ensure that it will work when needed.

Pepper spray can be a deterrent for aggressive dogs. If you jog, carry it, both for aggressive dogs and possible troublemakers. Some states may require training and a permit for possession and use of pepper spray. Some may also have regulations regarding its use. Do your research. Where I live, it can be purchased as a bear deterrent. Same ingredients, just a bigger container.

Firearms – I believe in a person's right to carry a firearm for protection. I also believe that a person intending to do so should first have a thorough understanding of all aspects of using a firearm for personal defense. The legal right to use deadly force is necessary. But any person thinking of using a firearm for protection also needs to understand its limitations in disabling another. Hollywood routinely shows an assailant becoming instantly, and completely, disabled when shot. Sometimes even being thrown backwards. Simple physics disproves this fallacy. If there were enough energy in a bullet's impact to force a person to fly backwards, the equal and opposite reaction would force the shooter backwards as well. Instantly disabling another by gun shot is a rare occurrence. Unless a bullet strikes the spine, or certain parts of the brain, the assailant will most likely remain physically able to continue the attack until blood loss renders him unconscious. If he also has a firearm, he can return fire until he is disabled or passes out. Whenever you read or hear of a person getting shot, pay attention to when, if ever, the person dies. Usually, if it occurs at all, it is later, sometimes even days. The use of a firearm to instantly disable another is problematic.

You may think that just displaying a firearm will cause the other person to cease threatening behavior. In my experience, it doesn't necessarily work out like that.

The following incident happened when my partner and I were working a midnight shift. It occurred at the culmination of a high-speed pursuit on a two-lane country road. The chase included us getting forced off the road at a little over 100 miles an hour. The pursued eventually rolled his car three times when he failed to make a hairpin turn to the left. The car came to rest upright, in the middle of the roadway. The driver was lying half out of his car with his legs in the car and his torso on the pavement. He was bleeding from a large cut that extended from the center of his forehead to his hairline at the back his head. He was unconscious. As we removed him from the vehicle, my partner severely cut his left hand on a piece of glass. He returned to our car to bandage his cut. Just as I managed to bandage the miscreant's head, he came to. He then stood up, and with his back to the open car door, decided to fight.

"Alright, enough nonsense", I thought. I unholstered my pistol and pointed it at him. He was a lot bigger than I was. It seemed like a good idea at the time. He should have given up, right? He responded by saying "Oh, so you want to play with guns!" He then turned and reached under the drivers' side car seat. At the same instant, I noticed pistol ammunition lying about on the roadway. No, no one got shot, but the subsequent fight was pretty exciting for my partner and me.

As it turned out, the subject had no criminal record and even had a clean driving record. The next day, from his hospital bed, the driver apologized to us. He said he ran from us as he was doing about 100 miles an hour when he first saw us and decided to try to outrun us. He claimed no memory of wanting to fight or reaching for a firearm. He said he didn't intend to

> *run us off the road, but had apparently turned his wheel to the left when he looked over at us. He wasn't what you might think of as a "bad guy". He was just someone who made several poor decisions at the time. He had been drinking but not so much that he was legally drunk. He was less than 25 years old. Do you suppose that his incomplete pre-frontal cortex had anything to do with his poor decision making?*

Because of this incident, I don't believe that displaying a firearm, as a bluff, is a good idea. If the need is there to shoot, fine, but I don't recommend using a firearm as a bluff. Besides, if you point a firearm at another, that person may be legally justified in using a firearm against you. You would be threatening deadly force whether or not you intended to shoot.

CONCLUSION

I believe the way to prevent an abduction is to have the ability to protect yourself. You must do everything possible to avoid being taken to a second location. Martial arts would be my first choice. You only need to be proficient enough to prevent another from controlling you, and to know how to break away. Learning enough martial arts to be able to throw an assailant to the ground would be a bonus. Stun devices and pepper spray would be my next choice. A well-trained dog is a great option but wouldn't always be available. Using a firearm would be my last choice.

Anytime there is a risk of a carjacking or of an abduction, no matter how slight, you need to remain aware of others around you. Maintain your "bubble" just as you would when driving. Who is approaching you from behind, the front, from either side? Your personal bubble needn't be large, just large enough to see anyone that can be within reach of you within a few seconds. Move away from persons who make you uncomfortable. Do not use your phone or listen to music with ear buds when you are vulnerable. Use all your senses to protect yourself.

Practice Anticipation and Visualization for both carjackings and abductions. How should you react? Should you fight? Use pepper spray or a stun device? Should you run, yell for help, act crazy and drool? All of these? Have a plan for each scenario. If you ever are in a situation requiring action, you won't waste precious time deciding what to do, or worse, freezing instead of fighting or fleeing.

Chapter 12

SOME MISCELLANEOUS THOUGHTS

POLICE OFFICERS

IF YOU ARE STOPPED by a Police Officer, State Trooper or Highway Patrolman, there are a couple of things you can do to make the stop safer for both you and the officer. First, always try to stop as far as you can from the traveled portion of the roadway. In town, try to pull into a parking lot or driveway. Avoid stopping in the roadway. If that means traveling a bit before stopping, use your signal while slowing down to let the officer know you are complying. Officers will generally put on their lights only when there is a safe place for you to pull over. If on a highway, again signal, and then pull off the roadway as far as is practical.

Passing motorists will turn to look at the scene. A police officer stopping a motorist is always of interest to most folks. Remember when we discussed that some drivers will turn the steering wheel slightly in the direction where they are looking? Occasionally this will result in that vehicle driving into the stopped patrol car, the officer, or your vehicle. Give yourself and the officer the most room possible away from moving traffic. It is safer for you both. ,

Next, and very important, keep your hands where the officer can see them while she is approaching. Place yourself in the officer's position. She doesn't know how you will react. She doesn't know if you are a dangerous person. If you reach into a glove compartment or under your seat you could be getting out your registration or you could be reaching for a weapon. You could be trying to hide drugs. She doesn't know what you are doing nor your intent. Help put the officer at ease.

As a driver, keep your hands in full view as she approaches. Keeping them on the steering wheel is a good indication to the officer that you mean no harm. As for your passengers, tell them likewise to keep their hands in view and not make any suspicious moves. Passengers should remain still and not move about. They should not reach into anything that could contain a weapon, such as a purse. Your passenger may only want to take a picture of you getting a citation to show to your friends. The officer has to assume that the passenger may be reaching for a weapon. To assume otherwise would be risky. Once the officer contacts you, if asked for documents, tell the officer where they are before reaching for them.

It also helps to be polite. If you are going to get a warning rather than a ticket, being confrontational will pretty much eliminate that outcome. You have probably heard that police officers have a "quota" for writing tickets. In my 28 years with various police agencies, I have never seen it. It might exist somewhere but I have never seen it nor heard of it as a requirement. That means that officers probably have the discretion to write a ticket, issue a warning or let you go. Be polite. It just might save you a few dollars. Some departments may have a policy of writing a ticket for all stops involving violations. If that is the case, you probably will get a citation. But being polite might just get you a minor equipment citation instead of whatever it was you were doing.

FLAT TIRE

Tires have been vastly improved over the years. Well-maintained tires will go many miles without losing any air much less going flat. However, you could run over a nail or piece of sharp metal that will cause a flat tire. If you experience a flat tire and you are on a freeway, highway or other high-speed roadway, slow down and look for a safe place to pull way off the roadway. But don't do so where there is little chance of help arriving within a short time. You can drive a long way on a flat tire, miles if necessary.

You have probably seen videos of actual police chases where the fleeing miscreant continued to drive after one or more tires have been flattened by spikes deployed by police officers. You can even drive on the rim after the tire is completely shredded. You may need to replace the rim and the tire afterwards, but that is a cheap price to pay for being able to drive to a safe place to stop. You should not stop on a shoulder that is just wide enough to fit your vehicle. Having high speed traffic passing by within two or three feet is just too dangerous.

DISABLED VEHICLE

If your vehicle becomes disabled, pull over as far as you can onto the shoulder or even onto any area beyond. Turn on the four-way flashers and then get away from the vehicle. Do not stand behind the vehicle to "wave off" passing vehicles. If the oncoming drivers can't see your vehicle, they sure won't see you. You won't be helping them and you will be putting yourself in danger of serious injury or worse. There have been many incidents of motorists crashing into vehicles stopped in the roadway as well as on the shoulder. You don't want to be anywhere near if that happens.

ACCIDENTS

When I attended the New York State Police Academy, we were taught to first "protect the scene". This meant placing our vehicle behind the accident scene to protect it from oncoming traffic and then set out flares or other warning devices. Only then were we to help the injured. It would be of little benefit to anyone at the scene if we were to first focus on the injured only to have an oncoming vehicle crash into the accident scene, further injuring or killing the victims along with the officers.

Often, when arriving at an accident, I would find folks, both injured and uninjured, walking about on the roadway. Sometimes they would be disoriented or just talking to others. You need to get off the roadway quickly. If your vehicle is drivable, get it off the roadway. You will hear some say to leave the vehicles in place so that the investigating officer can better figure out exactly what happened. This might be practical if in town where traffic will stop almost instantly. But on high-speed roadways leaving the vehicle where it might be struck again by another vehicle is a bad idea.

Modern accident investigative techniques, using debris, marks in the roadway and damage to the vehicles should be sufficient. Besides you will still be alive to explain what happened. Leaving your vehicle in place and possibly causing secondary accidents is too risky. It is quicker and safer to drive your vehicle off the roadway than it is to get out and walk off.

If your vehicle isn't drivable, get away from it as quickly as possible. If the lights still work on your vehicle leave them on, especially the four-way flashers. Then move to a location off the roadway and away from oncoming traffic. If an oncoming vehicle does crash into your disabled vehicle, you will not risk injury from flying debris.

Many drivers have first aid kits in their vehicles. It is a good idea. Most automotive first aid kits are useful only for minor cuts and scratches. If you are going to carry one, include items such as large pressure bandages and medical grade tape, useful for serious injuries. Keep it in a readily available place.

AIR BAGS

Air bags inflate in a few thousandths of a second and then deflate. Any object in the path of the airbag will be forced outward, towards the occupant, with tremendous force. Occupants should not have any hard object between themselves and the airbags if there is any chance of an accident. Recently I saw a young girl, in the right front

220

passenger seat, with her feet resting on top of the dash. Imagine what would happen if the dash airbag inflated while she was in that position. In a few milliseconds, her legs would be forced upwards and towards her chest and head. Airbags can save lives but they can also be dangerous. Feet should remain on the floor. Also, ask grandma not to knit, or hold fido, while in the front passenger seat.

CONCLUSION

AS YOU CAN SEE, what started out as a collection of a few notes for my grandchildren has evolved into something more. This manual is longer and more complicated than I anticipated. There is a lot of information here. Perhaps too much to remember with one reading. So, let's try a listing of the key ideas for staying safe while driving.

- ✓ Drive only when rested – wide awake and no drugs or alcohol.
- ✓ Minimize driving in bad weather, at night, on two-lane roadways.
- ✓ Stay focused on driving - no distractions.
- ✓ Stay calm – promise yourself you won't get upset when another driver does something stupid.
- ✓ Brake before turns – no hard braking while turning.
- ✓ Always take the safer alternative.
- ✓ Distance yourself from potential hazards – both drivers and vehicles.
- ✓ Use the two-second rule to maintain distance.
- ✓ Be aware of everything in your "bubble".
- ✓ Practice "what if"
- ✓ Anticipate other drivers' actions.

223

✓ Leave yourself an out — someplace to go should a hazard present itself.

✓ Don't ride with unsafe drivers or in unsafe vehicles.

I have a laminated checklist for launching my boat. It is to ensure that I don't forget the important things, like installing the drain plug. I keep it over the visor in my truck. You might want to do the same for this list as a ready reminder before driving.

When you are finished with this manual please share it with, or pass it on to, another teen. If your parents haven't read this manual, have them at least read the following paragraph.

NOTE TO PARENTS

You need to be actively involved in your teen's driving education. Ride with them. Give them the benefit of the knowledge that you have gained over the years. Provide them with the best driver training you can find. I recommend that your teen attend a professional driving school specially designed for teens. Bondurant's "Advanced Teenage Driving" course in Phoenix, Arizona comes to mind. There are others.

Conclusion

Your teen will learn how to handle a vehicle in emergency situations in the safety of a training program, not on the road. I know that there is a cost for this professional training and money can be a factor. State laws mandate that you carry motor vehicle insurance for any injuries or damage you might cause. That insurance is primarily for the benefit of others. The cost of professional driving training for a teen is insurance to help keep your teen alive. The best insurance you could possibly buy. Then, after your teen has received adequate experience and is ready to drive, put him or her in the safest vehicle you can find. It doesn't have to be new, pretty or get great gas mileage. It just needs to be safe.

Conclusion

GLOSSARY

ABS –Anti-lock braking system: Sometimes called anti-skid braking system. A vehicle safety system that maintains traction between the tires and the road while braking by preventing the wheels from locking up. It does this by alternately applying and releasing some or all of the individual wheel brakes many times a second. It generally makes a pretty loud noise when doing so.

ACC – Adaptive Cruise Control: This system, using lasers, radar and cameras, or a combination, is designed to maintain a constant, safe following space between your vehicle and the one to the front.

Acceleration Skid – Loss of tire traction due to over accelerating

AEB – Automatic Emergency Braking: If this system senses a potential collision, and you don't react in time, it starts braking for you.

Autonomous Vehicle – A vehicle that drives by itself without input from the driver.

Barrier – Also see Jersey barrier - A modular wall or barrier, commonly made of concrete but sometimes plastic, to separate or redirect lanes of traffic.

Bias Ply Tires – An older tire design still available for classic cars. The cords of the tire run parallel with the direction of tire rotation. Still used on trailers for their weight-carrying abilities and resistance to swaying.

Blind Spot – A view over the driver's right shoulder towards the right rear of the vehicle. The driver cannot see what is in the blind spot due to vehicle design. Vehicle design intended to increase rollover protection has, in some vehicles, resulted in a larger blind spot due to larger roof support columns. Larger front roof-support columns have created blind spots to the front in some vehicles. Because the columns in front are closer to the driver the blind spots are smaller.

Blocker – A vehicle in the next lane over in an intersection, used as protection from being hit by a red-light runner from that direction.

Bluff Stop – A driver's action when arriving at an intersection where he is required to stop but appears to be driving too fast to do so. Generally, the driver will slam on the brakes and make the stop, but the bluff stop forces oncoming traffic to slow down to avoid being struck.

Braking Distance – The distance a vehicle will travel before stopping once the brakes are fully applied.

BSW – Blind-Spot Warning: This system warns of vehicles alongside your vehicle that you may not be able to see. It gives a visual, audible and/or tactile warning that it is unsafe to merge or change lanes. The tactile warning may be a vibration in the steering wheel or seat.

Bubble – An imaginary area around a moving vehicle, generally in the shape of an oval, within which a driver should be aware of all other vehicles and other potential hazards.

California Stop – When a vehicle rolls through a stop sign or red light rather than coming to a complete stop. Most common when the vehicle is making a right turn. Also known as a California roll.

Collision Avoidance System – An electronic safety system using radar, cameras and/or laser to sense an impending accident and avoid it. There are several different systems in place and being developed as this manual is being written. Some give audible and/or visual warnings while others take autonomous action by applying the brakes and/or steering.

Crashworthiness – A measure of a vehicle's ability to absorb the energy of a collision to prevent, or at least minimize, intrusion of structural components of the vehicle into the passenger compartment. Both NHTSA and IIHS rate vehicles based upon their crashworthiness.

Crumple Zone – That part of a vehicle designed to absorb the energy of a collision to prevent, or at least minimize, intrusion of structural components of the vehicle into the passenger compartment.

Drifting – A skid where the rear wheels have lost traction while the front have not, causing the vehicle's rear to slide to the right in a left turn, and to the left in a right turn.

Driver Assistance System – Also known as ADAS, Advanced Driver Assistance System. On-board vehicle systems designed to avoid collisions by providing the driver with alerts of potential collisions; to stay in one lane; and/or by actively taking over control of the vehicle just long enough to avoid a collision. Features include adaptive cruise control, braking, steering, incorporation of gps, and numerous other technologies. This is different than the autonomous vehicle system whereby the vehicle controls all the driving.

ESC – Electronic Stability Control: See explanation for VSC.

FCW – Forward Collision Warning: This system will activate when it senses an impending collision with an object or vehicle directly in front. It may provide a visual, audible ad/or tactile alert.

Footprint – That portion of the tire that contacts the roadway.

Hotdog – A hazardous driver that constantly changes lanes, speeds and tailgates.

Hydroplane – A loss of steering or braking control when a layer of water prevents direct contact between tires and the road.

I.I.H.S. – Insurance Institute for Highway Safety: A non-profit organization funded by insurance companies. Its purpose is to reduce the severity of vehicle crashes, and to minimize injuries and property damage caused by the accidents. The crash test results are available on its website.

Inertia – The resistance of any physical object to a change in its speed and/or direction. It is the tendency of objects to continue moving in a straight line at a constant velocity.

Inside Lane – On multiple-lane highways, the lane on the left, next to the center of the roadway.

Jersey Barrier – A concrete barrier, generally 32" tall, designed to separate lanes of traffic. Used at road construction sites to temporarily reroute traffic. Sometimes used as permanent barriers between lanes of opposing traffic. Occasionally made of plastic. A 42" tall version is known as the Ontario Tall Wall.

Joules – A unit of measurement of the kinetic energy of a moving object. A moving vehicle will have a certain amount of kinetic energy which must be used up/absorbed, before it can be stopped.

Kinetic Energy – The amount of energy a moving object has due to its motion.

Lagging Left Turn Signal – The left turn signal at an intersection will come on after the green signal for through traffic.

LDW – Lane Departure Warning: This system, using visual, audible and/or tactile warnings, will alert you when you cross over lane markings, unless your turn signal is on.

Leading Left Turn Signal – The left turn signal at an intersection will come on before the green signal for through traffic.

LKA – Lane-Keeping Assist: This system will provide steering and braking input if you are changing lanes while your turn signal is not activated. Notice the difference with an LDW system, which only warns but does not take control of steering and brakes.

Magnetic Driver – The driver of a vehicle that approaches another moving vehicle and then matches its speed. The result is that the two vehicles continue traveling at the same speed, while close to one another. Typically, the magnetic driver will stay in the other vehicle's blind spot.

Mass – For the purposes of this manual, mass means the same as the weight of a vehicle.

Momentum – The product of the mass and the velocity of an object.

N.H.T.S.A. – National Highway Transportation Safety Administration: An agency of the federal government. Its mission is "reducing deaths, injuries and economic losses resulting from motor vehicle crashes". It conducts vehicle crash tests and provides the results on its website.

Outside Lane – On multiple-lane highways, the lane on the right.

Oversteer – A term of vehicle dynamics which describes what occurs when a vehicle turns sharper than intended. Generally caused by a driver turning the steering wheel too much for the speed being driven. Oversteering can result in a drifting skid and a possible rollover;

Perception Time – The time it takes a driver to perceive a possible hazard.

Pilot Vehicle – A vehicle that is followed to "see" what is further ahead than the driver can see. It is a vehicle that one would follow at a distance, when on an unfamiliar road, to give notice of turns and dips in the roadway as well as potential hazards that cannot yet be seen. A pilot vehicle is of particular use on unlighted, unfamiliar, two lane roadways, during the nighttime hours.

Pothole – A hole in the road surface, generally caused by water and freezing weather.

Radial Ply Tire – A newer design of tires where the plies of the tire are at 90 degrees to the direction of travel. Used on most, if not all, modern passenger vehicles. A radial ply tire provides better steering control and tread life than the bias ply tire.

RCTW – Rear Cross-Traffic Warning: This system gives a visual, audible and/or tactile warning of an object or vehicle that is out of rear camera range but is in your path as you are backing.

Reaction Time – The time it takes a driver to react to a perceived need to either brake, turn or accelerate. One of the three components of Stopping Distance.

Rolling Billboard – A vehicle in front that blocks a driver's view to the front of that vehicle. Common examples would include motor homes, tractor-trailers and other large trucks.

Self-Driving System – The electronic system used in an autonomous vehicle. It requires no input from a driver other than inputting the destination.

Skid – When one or more tires have lost traction with the road surface.

Stopping Distance – The total distance to stop a vehicle. It consists of three variable components: perception time, reaction time, and braking distance.

TCS – Traction Control System: A safety system that prevents the wheels from losing traction when driving on a slippery road surface. It uses wheel sensors to detect when one drive wheel is turning faster than another. Traction control and ABS are part of the stability control systems the federal government has required since 2012.

Turbulence – The flow of air around a moving vehicle. Turbulence caused by a larger vehicle like a tractor-trailer can "push" a lighter vehicle away from its direction of travel, causing it to lose traction, especially on snow-covered or wet roadways.

Two Lane Roadway – One lane in each direction, separated only by pavement markings.

Two Second Rule – An old rule of thumb whereby a driver can maintain a safe driving distance without having to calculate various stopping distances for any given speed. A driver simply drives two seconds behind the vehicle in front. The driver selects a spot in the roadway as the vehicle in front passes it and then counts one thousand one, one thousand two. If the driver reaches that same spot at or after two seconds, the distance between the two vehicles is considered adequate, assuming good roads and dry weather. At nighttime, in inclement weather, or traveling downhill, a greater distance may be required for safety. I suggest using a three-second rule and to add more time at night, in inclement weather and when descending a hill.

Understeer – A term of vehicle dynamics which describes what occurs when a vehicle turns less than intended. It is a function of the vehicle's design. Most passenger vehicles are designed with slight understeer. This provides a margin of safety from the risk of an oversteer, which can result in a drifting skid and overturning.

Visualization – A technique whereby one imagines encountering a certain situation and reacting to it in the best way possible. It is a tool to improve a driver's ability to react appropriately to hazardous driving situations before they are encountered.

VSC – Vehicle Stability Control: This system helps prevent wheels from skidding sideways when cornering or oversteering. It also helps by maintaining traction during hard braking. Sometimes called ESC – Electronic Stability Control.

Walkabout – To walk around a vehicle before getting into it to drive. A brief inspection of the vehicle by looking for anything unusual, such as a flat or under-inflated tire, leaking fluids or broken tail or headlights.

Weight shifting – The shifting of the weight from one tire to another. It is caused by braking, turning, accelerating and the attitude of the vehicle.

Weight – For the purposes of this manual, the terms weight and mass mean the same.

NOTES

NOTES

NOTES

Made in the USA
Columbia, SC
11 November 2020